AF258489

I'm Still Here

By

Lan Anh Nguyen

Lan Anh Nguyen

I'm Still Here

This is a nonfiction work. Events are portrayed as truthfully as memory allows. Some names and identifying details have been changed to protect the privacy of individuals.

Published in Australia by: Sydney Book Publishers

Cover design by: Lan Anh Nguyen & Sydney Book Publishers

Edited by Sydney Book Publishers

Printed in Australia

Paper Back.

E-Book.

I'm Still Here

I'm Still Here contains sensitive material related to sexual assault, domestic violence, and financial, emotional, physical, and psychological abuse. These experiences are shared with honesty and vulnerability as part of the author's journey towards healing and truth.

Some readers may find this content distressing or triggering. If you feel overwhelmed or upset at any point, please pause and seek support. You are not alone.

In Australia, you can reach out to:

- Beyond Blue, 1300 22 4636

- Lifeline, 13 11 14

- 1800RESPECT, 1800 737 732

Your well-being matters. Please take care of yourself as you read.

Lan Anh Nguyen

Table of Contents

Chapter 10

Chapter 11

Chapter 12

Chapter 13

Chapter 14

Chapter 15

Chapter 16

Chapter 17

Chapter 18

Chapter 19

Chapter 20

Introduction

I'm Still Here

Written by Lan Anh Nguyen.

This is not just a story.

It's survival. A reckoning. A rebirth.

I'm Still Here is the truth behind the smile I once had to fake. It's the voice I reclaimed after years of silence. It's the journey of a woman who endured betrayal, control, heartbreak, and fear, and still chose love, motherhood, and healing.

I've lived through two broken marriages, the weight of judgment, and the ache of raising children amid chaos. I've faced police interviews, courtrooms, stalking, and threats. I've fled homes, rebuilt lives, and stood in the fire to protect my children. And through it all, I never disappeared.

This book is my testimony.

It's the story behind my poems, my lyrics, my art. It's the reason I write with such emotional depth, because every word carries a scar, a memory, a triumph.

You'll meet the woman I was: exhausted, invisible, afraid.

You'll meet the mother I became: protective, resilient, fiercely devoted. And you'll meet the woman I am now: empowered, creative, and finally free.

You'll also meet the people who helped me rise, my children, my new partner, and his beautiful parents, who became my safe haven. Their love reminded me that healing is possible. That kindness still exists that I am worthy of joy.

This is not a perfect story.

But it's mine. And I'm still here.

About the Author

Lan Anh Nguyen

Lan Anh Nguyen is a Vietnamese-Australian writer, poet, and mother whose work is rooted in lived experience, emotional truth, and quiet resilience. I'm Still Here is her first book, a deeply personal memoir tracing her journey through heartbreak, survival, motherhood, and healing.

She writes with honesty and heart, drawing on the challenges she has faced and the strength she has found along the way. Her words resonate with anyone who has ever felt silenced, unseen, or afraid to begin again.

She lives in Melbourne with her children, where she continues to write, reflect, and rebuild a life filled with meaning, love, and hope.

I'm Still Here

By

Lan Anh Nguyen

Chapter 1

A Journey Of Courage: From War To Wonder

My earliest memories are of starting a new life on foreign soil. My parents, brave and determined, fled our homeland of Vietnam in search of peace, a dream that shimmered faintly beyond the chaos of war.

We packed only what we absolutely needed, one change of clothes each, a little food, a few bottles of water. Even those felt heavy, as if the weight of what we were leaving behind clung to every item we carried.

We slipped out in the middle of the night, our footsteps swallowed by the darkness. The cemetery was our only safe passage, a place where no one bothered to look. Gravestones rose around us like crooked teeth, their shadows stretching long and thin across the ground. The air was cold enough to sting, and every sound—every crunch of gravel, every rustle of grass—felt dangerously loud. It was the kind of silence that made you hold your breath without realising it.

As we reached the far edge of the graveyard, the darkness shifted. Shapes emerged dozens of them. At least fifty people were already gathered, clustered in tight groups, their faces pale in the moonlight. Mothers held their children close. Men whispered urgently to one another. Bags were clutched to chests as if letting go would mean losing everything. The tension in the air was thick, almost metallic, like the moment before a storm breaks.

Ahead of us, the boat waited—a small, battered thing that looked like it had survived too many journeys already. Its paint was peeling in long strips, and the wood groaned even while still tied to the post.

People lined up in a wavering, anxious line, shifting from foot to foot, glancing over their shoulders as if danger might appear at any moment.

The whispers around us were barely audible, just threads of fear carried on the wind. Someone shushed a crying child. Someone else muttered a prayer. The boat rocked gently in the dark water, as if impatient or warning us.

When our turn came, we stepped forward, careful not to stumble, careful not to draw attention. The boards creaked under our weight as we climbed in, joining the tightly packed crowd. Bodies pressed shoulder to shoulder, breath mingling in the cold night air. The boat felt impossibly small for so many of us, and yet no one dared complain.

As the last few people squeezed aboard, the night seemed to close in around us. The engine sputtered softly, and the boat drifted away from the shore—slowly, silently—carrying fifty souls into the darkness, each of us hoping the water ahead was safer than the land behind.

What began as a hopeful voyage toward peace and freedom quickly descended into a nightmare none of us could have imagined. In the darkness of the second unforgiving night, our boat was ambushed by pirates. They came at us with violence and greed, tearing away what little we had left—our food, our clothing, and even the last fragile pieces of dignity we tried so desperately to hold onto. The women on board endured horrors that still echo through our memories; some were assaulted, some women and children taken, and others lost their lives in acts of brutality that no sea could ever wash away.

My mother had clung to a few precious keepsakes—small tokens of her past, her identity, her story. Even those were taken from her. Perhaps it was those valuables, surrendered in desperation, that spared our family from an even worse fate. But the violence did not end with theft. I remember the terror as bodies were thrown overboard, the ocean swallowing every trace of cruelty and loss. Each wave seemed to carry away another piece of hope, another fragment of who we were.

What was meant to be a passage to safety and a new beginning became a journey marked by trauma, grief, and the kind of fear that settles deep into the bones. The promise of freedom was replaced by mourning, and the scars of that night followed us long after the horizon changed. We survived, but the memory of that crossing—its brutality, its sorrow, its stolen innocence—remains a shadow that time alone cannot erase.

I'm Still Here

We were given only two small sips of water, the size of a small lid on a bottle, each day for the entire journey. Our throats burned with thirst, our lips dry and cracked, splitting each time we tried to speak, our stomachs hollow from hunger. The heat, the stench, the endless days—everything pressed against us. People grew weak, then feverish. Some slipped into delirium; others simply closed their eyes and never opened them again. Those who didn't survive were carried to the edge and thrown overboard, their bodies disappearing into the water as if their suffering had never existed. It was a journey stripped of dignity, mercy, and hope—raw, unforgiving, and impossible to forget.

My parents' courage didn't begin with the escape; it was forged long before, in the quiet defiance of love.

My father was the eldest of nine children, a country boy raised in poverty. He left school early to help support his family, growing crops and living off the land. By eighteen, he had joined the army, carrying the weight of duty on his shoulders.

Dad's family lived by the tides.

They were fishermen, not by choice, but by necessity. Each morning, they pushed their boats into the surf, with nets neatly coiled at their feet, worn from years of use, ready for another day's work. The sea gave what it gave: sometimes plenty, sometimes nothing at all. They sold their catch in noisy markets and quiet villages, trading fish for coins, rice, or whatever people could offer. It was hard work.

Honest work. The kind that shaped their hands and their silence.

My mother, by contrast, grew up in Saigon with comfort and privilege. She was a city girl, sheltered and spoilt, with maids to cook and clean. She had never washed clothes or prepared a meal; everything was done for her.

They met by chance. Dad was selling desserts and drinks, travelling into the city to find better-paying customers. Mum became one of his regulars. That simple exchange, sweet treats, and quiet smiles, was the beginning of their love story.

Her parents disapproved. They feared poverty, the stark difference in lifestyle. But my parents were persistent. They married against the odds, and Mum stepped into a world she had never known. She learned to cook, to clean, to live simply. She didn't even know how to cook rice. But she tried. Slowly, she adapted.

Their love was not grand or easy; it was quiet, resilient, and real.

Dad had served as a soldier during the war, carrying not just duty but the trauma of conflict.

The final surrender came on April 30, 1975, when North Vietnamese forces entered the Presidential Palace in Saigon. With the war finally over, my parents longed for a life beyond fear and mere survival. They wanted a different future—one where their children could grow up safe, far from the echoes of gunfire and grief.

A few years after the war ended, that longing became a decision. They chose to leave everything behind. And in doing so, they chose hope.

After six long days and five nights adrift, we landed on a small island, Pulau Bidong, in Malaysia. The moment our feet touched sand, a wave of relief washed over us, joy mingled with exhaustion, as if the earth itself had opened its arms.

Mum had been heavily pregnant when we fled Vietnam, carrying not just fear and hope, but new life. My youngest sister was born on that island, her first cries mingling with the sound of waves and whispered prayers. That place became our temporary home for a year of waiting, healing, and quiet resilience.

Eventually, Australia opened its arms to us. We arrived with nothing but the clothes on our backs and the scars of survival etched into our hearts.

My parents had lost everything, but they never lost their will to rebuild. Without knowing a word of English, they worked tirelessly. My father found full-time work, while my mother stitched dreams into fabric, sewing from home and raising four daughters with grace and grit. I was the third child, nestled between the strength of my older sisters and the innocence of my younger one.

My mum eventually found full-time work sewing in a factory, and Dad continued working in a factory. Our days were simple, but never easy. We walked to school, came home, and prepared dinner before our parents returned from work. One sister would wash the vegetables, another would start the rice, and the eldest would stir something fragrant on the stove. We had just fifteen or twenty minutes to eat before we joined Mum and Dad in sewing moccasins, jewellery pouches, anything that could help us save for our first home and support family still overseas.

We didn't have much. But we had each other. And somehow, that was enough.

Life was tough, happiness didn't look grand or polished for us, but it was threaded with love, laughter, and the quiet joy of small victories. We were happy in our own way. The world outside may not have understood our language, but inside our home, every stitch, every shared meal, every sacrifice spoke volumes.

Chapter 2

Childhood In Bloom: Nature, Play, And Becoming

We didn't have toys growing up, not the kind you'd find in glossy catalogues or behind glass shop windows, but we had imagination. I made daisy chains from wildflowers, collected smooth stones and turned them into treasures, built muddy cakes and served them to invisible guests. The earth was my playground, and nature was my companion.

Our backyard was a kingdom of plum and apple trees. I loved climbing high into their branches, feeling the wind kiss my cheeks as I perched above the world. I dreamed of building a treehouse there, a secret place where stories could unfold and birdsong would be my lullaby.

As the third daughter in a family that longed for a son, I was dressed in boys' clothes until I was nine. It wasn't cruel, it was practical, cultural, perhaps even hopeful. I didn't mind. I played sports with the boys at school, ran fast, climbed trees, and felt strong. I belonged in that world of rough-and-tumble games and scraped knees.

Dad worked tirelessly. His hands were always busy, fixing, building, providing. His love was quiet but steady, stitched into every sacrifice.

One day, he came home with a surprise. He called my sisters and me outside, his voice carrying rare excitement. There it was, a tricycle. Our very first toy. It was blue, with a bright red horn that squeaked when pressed. On the back was a small basket, my treasure chest. I'd fill it with wildflowers and smooth stones, collecting beauty wherever I found it. All four of us shared that tricycle, taking turns, racing down the dirt path, laughing until our bellies hurt.

I was inventive, sometimes mischievous. I'd collect small objects, even insects like bees, and fire them out of the horn like a cannon. Looking back, I know it was cruel. I stopped the day I got stung. My foot swelled tight and hot, a painful lesson learned.

That tricycle was the only toy we owned. But Dad made magic out of nothing. He built a swing from wood and rope and tied it to the big apple tree in our yard. I loved that swing. It creaked when I soared, the wind rushing past my ears, the leaves whispering stories above me.

I made my own bow and arrows too, sticks sharpened, string tied tight. I'd play shooting games against the fence, imagining I was a warrior, strong and brave. In those moments, I felt free. I felt powerful. I felt like anything was possible.

But by eleven, something shifted. My body began to change, and with it came confusion. Breasts began to grow, and I didn't know how to feel about them. I wasn't ready. I tried to hide them, strapping them down, layering clothes to disguise what felt unfamiliar and unwanted. It was a quiet struggle, one I carried alone, wrapped in fabric and silence.

These years were a bridge between childhood and womanhood, between freedom and self-awareness. They were tender, tangled, and formative. And through it all, I remained that girl who loved the trees, the birds, the mud pies, and the daisy chains, still searching for a place to belong, still dreaming of a treehouse in the sky.

Chapter 3

The Music Stopped: A Shattered Morning

As the years passed, our home filled with more than just the hum of sewing machines and the clatter of dinner plates; it filled with music.

Dad would cradle his guitar like a second heart, his fingers dancing across the strings as melodies poured into the room. My sisters and I would gather around, memorising lyrics, harmonising with laughter, our voices rising like birdsong. Even after long days of work and school, the weekends were sacred, woven with music, joy, and the warmth of newfound friendships. We didn't have much, but we had rhythm, and we had each other.

But one weekend, the music stopped.

It was a Sunday night. One of Dad's close friends had stayed too long, drank too much. My parents, kind and trusting, offered him the couch to sleep it off, a gesture of care, something you do for someone you consider family.

Monday morning came. We woke up early, as always, to get ready for school. But something was wrong. My eldest sister was gone. So was Dad's friend.

Panic set in like a storm cloud. We searched the house, calling her name. Nothing. My parents, usually calm and composed, were frantic. We ran across the street to our neighbours, one of the few families who spoke English, and they called the police.

The hours that followed were a blur of sirens, questions, and silence. I remember the look on my parents' faces, etched with fear, disbelief, and something deeper. Something breaking.

My sister had been missing for two long days before the police finally found her. When they brought her home, the air in our house shifted. Relief and devastation arrived together, tangled in the same breath. I remember the sound of the front door opening, the heavy footsteps of the officers, the way my mother's cry broke through the silence like glass shattering. My father stood rigid, his face carved in stone, as if holding himself together was the only thing he could do.

The police carried a clear plastic bag. Inside were my sister's underwear and bra. I didn't understand what it meant. I was too young, too innocent. But I knew something terrible had happened. My sister's eyes looked far away, as if she had left part of herself behind in those two days.

My sister had been taken, hurt, and violated by someone my parents had welcomed into our home. Someone they trusted.

The police made an arrest. The man who had hurt her was not a stranger. He had been welcomed into our home, trusted by my parents, and allowed to sit at our table. And in that trust, he had found his way to violate something sacred.

No one explained anything to me. No one told me why the bag mattered, why my sister's silence felt heavier than words. I only knew that the house itself seemed changed—its walls thinner, its air colder, its safety gone.

I learned, in that moment, that evil does not always come from outside. Sometimes it walks through the front door, welcomed, smiling, carrying gifts. Sometimes it wears the face of someone you thought you knew.

In that moment, something inside our family fractured. My parents, once our anchors, seemed to drift into a sea of grief and guilt. And though we were still together, something had been lost, something that music and laughter could no longer reach.

After my sister's trauma, an incident that shook the very foundation of our family, everything changed. The air in our home grew heavier and quieter. My sisters and I, still so young, instinctively turned inward. We didn't know how to speak about what had happened, and we didn't want to cause our parents any more pain than they were already carrying.

There was no family meeting, no shared grief, just a quiet understanding that we were all hurting, and that the best way to protect one another was to say nothing at all. We became experts at hiding our sadness, our confusion, our fear. We smiled when we were supposed to, helped with chores, went to school, and came home as if everything were normal. But inside, we were splintering.

From a young age, we absorbed the unspoken rule: silence was how we survived. Pain was something to be tucked away, not spoken aloud. We didn't have the language for our suffering, and even if we did, we weren't sure anyone could bear to hear it. So, we carried it, quietly, separately, believing that was the only way to keep our family from falling apart.

Chapter 4

Drawing Through The Silence: Finding Light In Shadows

My parents were still with us, but something in them had gone quiet. After the trauma that shattered our family, they became emotionally unreachable, haunted by guilt, grief, and the weight of betrayal. My father, once the man who played guitar and filled our home with music, became angry. Not just at the man who hurt us, but at the world itself.

I remember waking in the middle of the night, the house cloaked in silence. I found Dad sitting alone in the kitchen, the light off, a drink in his hand. It was the first time I ever saw him cry.

His shoulders shook, and his face, usually stern and unreadable, was open, raw. In that moment, the façade of strength he always maintained crumbled, revealing the depth of his pain and vulnerability. The sorrow that had been quietly simmering beneath the surface finally broke through, exposing emotions he had long kept hidden from his family. It was as if the weight of everything that had happened was too much to bear, leaving him unable to mask his feelings any longer. The sight was both shocking and heartbreaking, a stark reminder that even the strongest among us can be deeply affected by tragedy.

I walked up to him and wrapped my arms around him. He didn't speak. He just cried. In that moment, I saw the man behind the anger. I saw his pain. And even though I was afraid of him sometimes, I understood him. I knew he felt helpless. And so did I.

School became my sanctuary. My teachers were kind, gentle, and curious about who I was. They asked how I was doing. They noticed my drawings. Art became my refuge, a place where I could speak without words. I saved every coin I could to buy my first set of Derwent pencils. They were precious to me. With them, I could sketch the feelings I didn't know how to say.

There were days in my childhood when I didn't want to leave school and go home. School felt like a refuge—a place where I could breathe, where the world made sense, where I felt genuinely safe. It wasn't just the lessons or the routine. It was the feeling of being noticed, understood, and valued in a way I didn't always experience elsewhere.

At school, I was free to speak without worrying about consequences or saying the wrong thing. I didn't have to measure myself or shrink to fit. I could be open, expressive, and fully myself, and that freedom felt like sunlight on my skin.

Those moments taught me early on what safety and recognition feel like—and how deeply a child can crave them. They shaped the way I understand connection, comfort, and the places where I feel most myself.

My diary became my confidant, my secret keeper. In its pages, I poured my heart out, grief, confusion, and hope.

My eldest sister bore the deepest scars. Our parents didn't know how to help her. Their way was silence. They avoided the pain, hoping it would fade. But it didn't. She had to face the courts, relive the horror, and watch as the man who hurt her was sentenced to ten years in prison. It wasn't enough. Nothing was.

She tried to take her own life. By Year 9, she couldn't continue in school.

She couldn't focus, couldn't read or write. And still, no help came.

We were children navigating trauma without a map. But somehow, I found a path, through pencils, through paper, through the kindness of teachers who saw me. My art became my voice. My diary became my lifeline. And in the quiet spaces where no one asked, I found a way to speak.

Chapter 5

A New House, A New Silence

By the time I turned twelve, Mum and Dad decided my sisters and I would attend an all-girls school. Maybe it was their growing distrust of men, a protective instinct born from pain. Maybe they thought it would keep us safe. But for me, it felt like a sudden shift, a world I no longer recognised.

I had always played with boys, raced them across fields, kicked football, and climbed trees. I loved sports, loved the freedom of movement, and laughter. Now, I was in high school, dressed in summer dresses and winter skirts, surrounded by unfamiliar faces and unfamiliar rules. I felt out of place. I missed my primary school. I missed my friends. I missed the version of myself that felt free.

After my sister's trauma, something shifted in our household. My father became visibly stricter with all of us. The rules tightened like a drawstring: no sleepovers, no school camps, nothing that meant being away from home overnight. At first, I noticed the change in tone more than the change in policy. His voice carried a new edge, not angry, but alert. Watchful.

I didn't protest. I didn't cry or plead to go where my friends went. Somewhere inside, I understood. His fear wasn't abstract; it had a face, a name, a wound. He wasn't punishing us; he was shielding us. Trying, in the only way he knew how, to build a fortress around his daughters.

I never resented him for it. If anything, I felt a quiet solidarity with his grief. I saw how he carried it, not just in his rules, but in his silences. He didn't explain much, but he didn't need to. I knew his restrictions came from love, from a desperate need to keep us safe in a world that had proven itself capable of harm.

Around the same time, we moved out of the government home we had rented for years. Mum and Dad bought their first house, a symbol of survival, of starting over. They wanted to leave behind the memories that haunted the old walls. The pain. The betrayal. The silence.

Dad started a garden, just like the one he had back in Vietnam. It wasn't fancy, but it was purposeful. He planted spring onions, lettuce, cucumbers, and herbs like basil and mint. Anything we needed to cook with, Dad planted. It was his way of reclaiming control, of nurturing something with his own hands, of feeding us not just with food, but with care.

I became his helper. I mowed the lawns, pulled weeds, and watered the garden. I knelt beside him with my hands in the dirt, feeling the soil crumble between my fingers, warm and alive. It grounded me. It grounded us. I watched tiny seeds disappear into the earth, then reappear weeks later as shoots, then leaves, then food. It felt like magic. But it was also work, patient, quiet work. And in that rhythm, something shifted.

Dad's mood softened. He stopped pacing the house like a storm cloud. He smiled more. He'd hand me the hose with a nod, like we were teammates. I saw the change in his eyes when he looked at the garden, like he was seeing life again, not just loss. It was a great feeling. I felt like I was getting my father back.

We found a connection through the garden. It became our shared ritual, our silent language. I learned to appreciate food, not just for its taste, but for the time and effort it took to grow. I watched Dad save seeds for the next season, careful and methodical. I saw how he collected grass clippings for compost, how he rinsed rice without wasting a single grain. Nothing was taken for granted.

The garden taught me more than biology. It taught me reverence. It taught me that healing doesn't always come in words; it can come in rows of green, in the scent of mint crushed between fingers, in the quiet pride of a man who once carried too much grief. It can come from the simple act of placing your hands in the dirt and trusting something will grow.

I had a mischievous streak as a child, one that often got me into trouble, though not without a few unforgettable laughs.

My three sisters and I shared a bedroom in our modest two-bedroom house, where space was tight. The room held two bunk beds, squeezed in side by side, with a single desk wedged between them, our shared station for homework, drawing, and whispered secrets. One wardrobe stood in the corner, its doors barely able to contain the clothes of four growing girls. It was a simple setup, but it was ours.

My younger sister slept on the bottom bunk, which made her the perfect target for one of my more memorable pranks.

One summer, the blood plums in our backyard ripened to a deep, juicy red. I couldn't resist their drama. I crept into our room early one morning and tucked a handful of ripe plums under her blanket, letting them nestle into the sheets like little time bombs.

When she woke up, her scream echoed through the house.

"I'm bleeding! I'm bleeding!" she cried, scrambling out of bed in a panic. Her sheets were stained crimson; her nightgown streaked with plum juice. She was convinced something terrible had happened. I, of course, was doubled over with laughter until Mum came in, took one look, and turned her fury on me.

Then came Dad. He didn't laugh. He didn't even raise his voice. He just looked at the ruined fruit and said, "We don't waste food in this house." That quiet disappointment stung more than any punishment. We'd been taught to respect what we had, especially food; every plum was a gift from the garden, not a toy for tricks.

I got into serious trouble for that one. The plum prank was never repeated, but it lives on as one of our most outrageous childhood stories, born from a room full of sisters, squeezed furniture, and endless imagination.

The new house was quiet, but it had something magical: big trees. A plum tree. An apple tree. Just like before. When I saw them, my heart leapt. It was the one thing that felt familiar, like a whisper from my childhood. I imagined climbing them again, sitting high in the branches, listening to the birds sing. I imagined building that treehouse I had always dreamed of.

In a world that kept changing, the trees remained constant, always there through every upheaval and new beginning. Under their broad branches, I discovered a place where time seemed to pause, and the world's chaos melted away into the gentle rustle of leaves and birds singing. The trees offered more than mere solace; they served as living symbols that strength and grace could thrive, even during life's most challenging moments. When I felt uncertain or alone, I'd gaze up at their limbs, reassured by their ability to adapt with each passing season and yet remain true to themselves. The trees quietly reminded me that, no matter how unpredictable life became, there was always room for hope and surprise.

Chapter 6

Snowy: A Gift Of Kindness

High school became a canvas for my passions. I thrived in the arts, drawn to the textures of woodwork and the mysteries of science. Biology fascinated me—how life unfolded in delicate systems—and psychology gave me language for emotions I had long carried in silence. I was the teacher's pet in nearly every subject, not because I tried to be, but because I loved to learn. My teachers saw that, and they nurtured it.

The art room was my sanctuary. At lunchtime, while others gathered in noisy circles, I sat quietly among brushes and paper, drawing whatever my heart whispered. My art teacher was gentle and generous. She was getting married and asked if I could make roses out of fabric for her wedding dress. She handed me the fabric with trust in her eyes, and I took it home, stitching each petal with care. It felt like being part of something beautiful.

One afternoon, as class ended, my teacher asked me to stay back. I was surprised—curious, unsure. The room emptied, and she pulled out a large black bin bag. My heart fluttered with wonder. She handed it to me and said, "Open it."

Inside was the biggest, softest white teddy bear I had ever seen. My first ever soft toy.

I burst into tears.

She looked at me gently and asked if I was okay. I couldn't speak—I just hugged Snowy, the bear with a dark brown bow around his neck, and held him close. That walk home was one of the happiest moments of my life. I cradled Snowy like a treasure, eager to place him on my bed, where he would sit like a guardian of joy.

Snowy was far more than a simple gift; he was a testament to the profound impact of kindness and recognition. To me, he embodied what it meant to be truly seen—not just as another student or a face in the crowd, but as the quiet girl who found solace in crafting delicate roses and losing herself in the world of art. Snowy reflected an unspoken understanding and love, proof that someone noticed the silent devotion I poured into every brushstroke and every careful stitch. In a world that so often pressed down with its uncertainties and burdens, Snowy became a beacon of light, a tangible reminder that tenderness and joy could exist even in the heaviest of times. His presence on my bed was like a silent affirmation: I mattered, I was cherished, and I was not invisible.

Chapter 7

The Weight Of Silence

A few years passed. My parents worked tirelessly—not only to pay off their mortgage but also to support family overseas. As the eldest son, my father carried a heavy burden, responsible for his siblings abroad as well as his own family here in Australia.

My mother had come from a well-off background, but after her father passed away, everything changed. My grandmother was left to raise the rest of the family alone, and life became difficult. My parents took on the responsibility of supporting Mum's side of the family in Vietnam, too. Eventually, they decided to sponsor two of Mum's brothers, hoping they could find work in Australia and build a better future.

We lived in a modest two-bedroom home, but there was a bungalow out back where both uncles stayed. They found work quickly, and life shifted. For so long, it had just been Mum, Dad, and us four girls. Now, the rhythm of our household changed.

One uncle left early for work, and the other did shift work. The younger uncle was sometimes home when we returned from school. There was something strange about him. I couldn't explain it, but I felt uneasy around him. I would sense him behind me, watching. His presence made my skin crawl.

One afternoon, I was in the pantry, hungry after school.

Suddenly, he grabbed my arm. I panicked and ran out of the house, heart pounding, with him chasing after me. I didn't understand why he did it—I just knew I was afraid. I never told my parents. I didn't want to worry them.

Years passed. I began to notice changes in my second-oldest sister. She became withdrawn, spending most of her time in the bedroom. She only came out for dinner, then retreated again. Even on weekends, she kept to herself. Something was wrong, but in our family, we didn't talk about things. We each carried our own struggles in silence.

When my sister finished university and secured a successful job, she was eager to move out and live independently. She never shared her address.

To this day, none of us know where she lives. She visited occasionally—once every few months—but for a long time, we didn't hear from her at all.

Then one day, she found the courage to speak. She had sought counselling and support to help her understand her childhood and begin healing from her trauma. She had been violated by the same uncle. The one our parents had trusted. The one they had welcomed into our home, believing he would help build a better life.

It was the hardest thing my sister had ever done, breaking her silence after so many years. And suddenly, everything made sense. Her isolation. Her need to leave. Her distance. She had been protecting herself the only way she knew how.

Chapter 8

The Unspoken Years

We never talked about what happened. Not then, not for years. In our family, silence was the glue that held everything together, fragile, invisible, and always at risk of cracking. We carried our pain like folded laundry, tucked away, stacked neatly, never questioned.

I learned early how to read the room. How to sense when something was off, even if no one said a word. My sister's silence was loud. Her absence was louder. And when she finally spoke, it was like a door creaking open in a house we thought was sealed shut.

She had found her voice through counselling, through years of solitude and self-work. She named what had happened. She named him. And in doing so, she gave me permission to revisit my own memories—not just the pantry, not just the chase, but the feeling of being watched, of being unsafe in my own home.

I didn't tell my parents then. Maybe I was protecting them. Maybe, after seeing how my eldest sister's assault shook our family, I learned to cope by staying silent—by carrying things alone. Or maybe I was protecting myself. Maybe I am still learning what it means to speak.

We were only children, yet somehow we became the protectors. While our parents worked tirelessly to build a life from sacrifice and survival, we learned to shield them from our pain. We didn't want to add to their burdens, so we carried our own—quietly, separately, each of us retreating into ourselves. There were no family meetings, no shared language for sorrow. Just four daughters growing up in the same house, each learning in her own way how to survive the silence.

Chapter 9

From Strength To Softness: Becoming Myself

In P.E., I made it into the female weightlifting championships of Victoria. It was a moment of pride—a recognition of my strength, my discipline, my drive. But when I asked my parents for permission to compete, they said, "Girls don't do weightlifting." It stung.

I had been their boy for so long. I mowed the lawn, helped Dad in the garden, washed the car, and joined him at the metal shop to weigh in cans for cash. If something heavy needed lifting, I was the one they called. But when it came to celebrating that strength publicly, I was told to step back.

I wanted to learn karate. I loved martial arts—the power, the grace, the control. My favourite show was Monkey Magic, and I adored Astro Boy. I used to dream of flying through the sky like him—vivid, soaring dreams that felt more real than waking life. In those dreams, I was free.

At fourteen and a half, I got my first job at a grocery store. Thursdays, Fridays, and Saturdays were market days—hectic, noisy, and full of life. I saved every dollar I earned, and my first purchase was a high-quality sketchbook. Art was still my sanctuary.

The store owner had two daughters who needed help with maths, so I began tutoring them. When things were quiet, I would go upstairs to teach and draw with them. They looked up to me like an older sister, and I cherished that bond. It was the first time I felt like I could nurture others—not just survive, but uplift.

By eighteen, Year 12 loomed with its heavy questions. What will you do? Who will you become? I was in Year 12—exhausted, determined, and holding on. School was hard, life was harder. But I kept going. I knew finishing Year 12 meant something. It meant I had made it through.

Dad had promised me a gift when I graduated.

"Anything," he said.

"Really? Anything?" I asked.

"Yes. Anything."

I knew what I wanted. I had always dreamed of having a puppy of my own. But Mum never liked pets. They were messy, noisy, and expensive. I understood. So when Dad asked, "Okay, what is it that you like?" I hesitated—but said it anyway.

"A puppy."

Mum didn't even pause. "No. You are not getting a dog. No."

I let the idea go. I didn't want to upset her. I knew it would not make her happy.

The week after I finished school, Dad came home early on a Friday. I had taken time off from my grocery store job to focus on exams, only working weekends. That day, he walked in and said, "Get in the car.”

Just the two of us. That never happened.

I was excited. I had no idea where we were going.

“Dad, where are we going?” I asked. “You’ll see when we get there,” he replied.

We arrived at a big shopping centre. We walked through the shops, and then Dad stopped in front of a pet store.

He turned to me and said, “Pick one.”

My eyes lit up. My heart raced.

“But Mum said no,” I whispered.

Dad smiled. “It’ll be okay. Let me explain to your mum. She will come around.”

Inside were four ginger Chihuahuas—tiny, trembling, impossibly cute. I couldn’t decide. They were all so sweet. But one looked at me with wide, curious eyes. I chose him.

I named him Kuno.

He cost A$350. Back then, A$350 was a lot of money—more than half of Dad’s weekly wage. I was happy, but I felt guilty. Dad worked so hard, and I knew what that money meant. But he didn’t hesitate. He gave me joy without condition.

Kuno was clever, protective, and full of personality. He followed me everywhere, always alert, always watching. I wasn’t allowed to take him into my bed, but sometimes I would sneak him in anyway—he was just too adorable. His tiny body curled beside mine, warm and safe.

Even Mum, who had never wanted a dog, began to soften. I saw her watching him, smiling at his antics. She never said it outright, but I could tell—Kuno had won her over. He brought laughter into our home. Lightness. Joy.

That day, I didn't just get a puppy. I got a companion. A best friend. A quiet joy that stayed with me through everything that came next.

Life at eighteen seemed extremely stressful, with so many important decisions to make about my future.

I loved art, but my parents didn't see it as a future. "Artists are poor," they said. "They only become famous after they die." It wasn't exactly inspiring. I considered teaching, even joining the police force. But I chose nursing, biology, anatomy, and science. Something serious. Something they might respect.

By the end of my first year at university, I knew it wasn't for me. The labs, the cadavers, the amputated limbs were too much. The smell lingered. The weight of it all pressed down on me.

So, I deferred.

And I found my way to beauty therapy.

It was anatomy, yes—but it was also art. Brushes, colours,

textures. I discovered the joy of transforming faces, of offering relaxation and care. Facials became rituals of healing. Makeup became a canvas. My passion bloomed.

Year 12 had asked me to choose a path. I didn't know then that the path would twist and turn, that it would lead me not just to a career, but to myself.

Chapter 10

First Journey Home

Growing up, I watched my parents work tirelessly, their determination woven into the fabric of our daily lives. I absorbed their rhythm early—life, I learned, meant hard work, resilience, and sacrifice. Most of my childhood followed that steady beat. I saved every dollar I could from part-time jobs, babysitting, and odd chores, tucking away each bit with a quiet hope. By the time I turned eighteen, I had enough put aside to afford my first overseas trip—a long-awaited return to Vietnam, my birthplace and the home of so many family stories.

Travelling with my parents, I spent three weeks reconnecting with relatives and rediscovering roots I had only heard about in stories. My heart felt especially drawn to my father's village—it was unembellished, raw, and achingly real. The reality hit me hard: no electricity, no running water, not even a proper toilet. Water came from a communal well, and showers were bracing, taken with quick splashes from a bucket. I became acutely aware of every drop I used, conscious that the same precious water served the entire household. My daily habits shifted as I adapted to a rhythm of life so different from my own, where nothing was wasted, and every resource mattered.

At night, my dad's family powered an old, boxy television with a sputtering generator. As flickering images lit the room, villagers—

young and old—gathered outside, pressing their faces to the windows, their eyes wide with curiosity and delight. They didn't have the luxury of electricity, but they had something richer: each other. In those evenings, I learned the value of simple joys and togetherness, how laughter and company could fill a space more completely than any modern convenience. I realised how much I'd been taking for granted back home—the security, the comfort, the abundance of everyday life.

After dinner, the children gathered outside and sang as they washed dishes under the open sky. I felt a sense of belonging as I watched, listened, and joined in their chorus. The simple act of sharing chores became a moment of joy and connection. Climbing coconut trees came naturally to me, a skill I'd practiced since childhood, and it made me feel at home in a place otherwise unfamiliar. Yet my freedom had boundaries—my parents' worries loomed large. They warned me not to wander, fearing that danger might find me, that I could be stolen away or held for ransom. That fear, inherited and real, kept my world small. I stayed close, venturing no further than the edge of the village.

Instead of sightseeing, I found meaning in giving. My father's family needed a new boat—their livelihood depended on fishing, the river their lifeline. Without hesitation, I gave them the money I'd brought, knowing it would make a difference in their daily lives. Helping them, even in a small way, filled me with a sense of purpose and gratitude. It was a gift that rippled outwards, alleviating worry and strengthening our bond.

That journey was transformative. It taught me to live simply, to cherish what I had, and to never take comfort or connection for granted. It wasn't the sights that left the deepest impression, but the feelings—the warmth of family, the joy of meals shared on the floor, the resilience of a village thriving without modern convenience. I returned home changed, carrying these quiet lessons deep within me. They shaped the way I saw the world and the kind of person I hoped to become.

Chapter 11

Blossoming On My Own: Beauty, Balance, And Blooms

After completing my beauty therapy course, I felt a pull toward something more complete—something that blended the elegance of beauty with the craft of hair. So, I enrolled in hairdressing, eager to expand my skills and offer a fuller experience to those I cared for.

One hot summer afternoon, fresh from college and flushed from the heat, I wandered into a shopping centre. I grabbed a drink from a small takeaway store and collapsed onto a bench, gulping it down as the warmth wrapped around me. Across from where I sat was a salon—sleek, inviting, and offering both hair and beauty treatments. I looked like a mess, but something stirred in me. I stood up, smoothed my clothes, and walked toward the desk.

"Are you looking for staff?" I asked.

The receptionist smiled. "Hairdressing or beauty?" "Beauty," I replied.

She asked me to take a seat. Ten minutes later, a lovely woman emerged and introduced herself. Before I knew it, I was in the staff room, having an impromptu interview. She offered me a two-week trial. I landed the job immediately.

It felt like fate.

I'm Still Here

I loved everything about it—the vibe, the people, the rhythm of the salon. The clients were warm and kind, and I felt like I had found my place. My passion. My purpose.

I worked five days a week at the salon, pouring my heart into every treatment. On Tuesdays, I volunteered at a primary school as an art teaching assistant, sharing my love of creativity with children. Sundays were devoted to my own business—friends, family, and wedding makeups. I built my clientele with care, one face at a time.

Weekends were a whirlwind of bridal beauty. I looked after so many gorgeous women, helping them feel radiant on their most special days. I felt proud of my work—confident, fulfilled, and deeply connected to the art of transformation.

I was earning well, saving money, and building something that felt truly mine. My brushes, my hands, my heart—they all had a place in this world I had create.

For six transformative years, I dedicated myself to the salon, not only refining my technical expertise but also nurturing my inner growth. Each day became an opportunity to deepen my artistry and connect with the people who trusted me. At the same time, I poured energy into my own business, lovingly cultivating a loyal clientele. These clients relied on my hands, my heart, and my vision to help them look and feel their best. When my boss announced her plans to launch a new salon devoted exclusively to beauty, I felt an irresistible pull toward the adventure it promised. The prospect of a fresh start, new challenges, and creative possibilities inspired me to follow her, ready to embrace the next chapter.

But with this new beginning came an unrelenting pace. The salon buzzed with activity, appointments filling up faster than we could manage, and the search for skilled staff seemed endless. I found myself darting between two beauty rooms, my days a blur of treatments and consultations. The expectations grew—clients would settle for nothing less than my personal touch, refusing to book with anyone else. I was entrusted to train new hires, but the responsibility weighed heavily on my shoulders. Lunch breaks vanished, replaced by hurried sips of coffee and fleeting rests in corners. The sense of joy that once propelled me began to slip away, overshadowed by exhaustion and the pressure to perform.

The fatigue became constant—a silent companion that dulled my spirit. My body ached, my creativity waned, and I realised I was losing the spark that had once fuelled my passion.

In a moment of clarity, I chose courage over comfort: I decided to leave. It was a deliberate, empowering step—not a reckless leap, but a thoughtful move toward reclaiming my wellbeing and creative spark.

Thankfully, I wasn't starting from scratch. Over the years, I had built a strong reputation, earned the trust of my clients, and fuelled my unwavering passion for the beauty industry. The world of beauty was constantly evolving, with new techniques and tools emerging every season—and I felt ready, more than ever, to grow alongside it.

Setting out on my own proved to be the most rewarding decision of my career. Independence gave me the flexibility I craved: I worked smarter, earned more, and finally had the space to breathe and imagine. The luxury of choosing my own hours and projects brought a sense of peace and fulfilment I hadn't realised was missing.

With this newfound freedom, another passion blossomed. I enrolled in a floristry course, drawn by the allure of petals and vibrant colours. Flowers had always spoken to me, their textures and hues mirroring the gentle beauty I aspired to create in my work and life. Immersing myself in floristry felt like a natural extension of my artistry—a way to cultivate joy and softness, both for myself and for those around me.

Beauty and blooms, brushes and petals—my world was becoming a lush garden, lovingly tended and flourishing with intention. Each day was a chance to nurture my purpose, blending creativity and care in everything I touched.

Chapter 12

Roses And First Chances

At this season of my life, everything seemed to fall perfectly into place. My days were a harmonious blend of work, study, and creativity, and I relished a quiet sense of accomplishment that brought me genuine pride. I moved through each day with balance and contentment, grateful for the peace I had created for myself. When I began my floristry course, I was fortunate to meet a wonderful friend whose warmth and enthusiasm made every class a joy. She quickly became a source of both encouragement and inspiration. We bonded over shared stories, laughter, and our mutual passion for petals, stems, and the artistry of arranging blooms. Our friendship added new colour and joy to my world, deepening my appreciation for the beauty and connection that flowers and people can bring.

One afternoon, during arranging peonies and eucalyptus, she curiously asked if I was seeing anyone. I admitted I wasn't—my focus had been entirely on my education and career, leaving little room for romance. To me, dating felt somewhat distant, almost like a pursuit reserved for others. Despite my polite refusals, she would often mention her brother, insisting that we had to meet, and continually inviting me to join her family for dinner. I hesitated, uncertain and somewhat reluctant, gently declining her invitations time and again.

But then, on a whim, I agreed. I said yes.

<h3 style="text-align:center">I'm Still Here</h3>

The evening of the dinner, I arrived at her home feeling equally nervous and intrigued. Her brother greeted me at the door—tall, handsome, and well spoken, he immediately put me at ease with his genuine kindness. Unexpectedly, he wasn't alone; his friend had joined for dinner as well. The atmosphere was a tad awkward at first, but as the evening unfolded, laughter and impromptu karaoke filled the room, dissolving any tension. What began as an uncertain gathering soon turned into a night of light-hearted fun, spontaneity, and sweetness that I hadn't anticipated.

Just two days later, my phone rang with an unexpected call—from her brother's friend. I was genuinely surprised, having not shared my number with him. As it turned out, both men had asked for my contact information, but her brother's friend had been quicker to call. He explained that he wanted to get to know me better, his tone earnest and hopeful.

I'll admit, there wasn't an immediate spark. I wasn't particularly drawn to him, but I didn't wish to be impolite. I thought perhaps it was worth giving him a chance—after all, I didn't have a checklist for the "right" man, only a hope that he would be genuine, kind, and honest.

When he asked me out, he arrived with an armful of roses—several bunches, each a different colour because, as he confessed, he wasn't sure which I liked best. The gesture was thoughtful and endearing, touching me more deeply than I expected. As our day together unfolded, I found myself relaxing. He spoke animatedly about his love of fish and his flourishing aquarium, and to my delight, he adored orchids—one of my own favourite flowers. Over the course of our conversation, we discovered common interests and a shared appreciation for the gentle beauty of nature. What began as a tentative connection gradually grew into something sincere and promising.

Slowly, we began to see more of one another. Our relationship unfolded in a gentle, unhurried way—new yet comforting. My parents, ever protective, maintained strict curfews, which meant I had to be home by a certain hour. Within those boundaries, something quietly beautiful began to blossom: a connection rooted in curiosity, kindness, and growing companionship. Each day, the possibility of something lasting and meaningful took root, nurtured by patience and shared discovery.

Chapter 13

A Promise And A Pivot: When Dreams Meet Destiny

By the time I turned twenty-six, I felt as though I were poised on the brink of something truly extraordinary. My beauty business was thriving, and each day brought new excitement as I watched it blossom into a unique reflection of my vision and values. At the heart of my dreams was an ambitious idea—a salon that would seamlessly blend beauty with the natural elegance of flowers, a florist café where creativity and nature could mingle in perfect harmony. I pictured vibrant colours splashed across the walls, the scent of fresh blooms weaving through the air, and customers lingering over coffee amidst lush floral arrangements. My imagination ran wild with possibilities: textures, palettes, and experiences that would make my business not just a place of transformation, but a haven for inspiration. Every step forward felt deeply personal, as though I were building a sanctuary that belonged solely to me, nourished by my passion and purpose.

During this flurry of growth and planning, my boyfriend was charting his own course, though not without difficulty. He was finishing his final year at university, balancing the pressures of study with a job in a warehouse that drained his spirit and left him feeling restless and unfulfilled. Even once he graduated, he remained in that role, unable to break free from the comfort and security it offered, yet longing for something more meaningful. I often watched him struggle, wishing I could ease his frustration or help him find clarity about his path. There were moments when I wondered how our journeys might converge—whether my momentum would carry us forward together, or pull us in separate directions. The uncertainty lingered, leaving me unsure how to support him while still nurturing my own burgeoning ambitions.

And then, in the midst of these swirling questions and restless days, he proposed. It was unexpected—not because I didn't care for him or see a future with us, but because I hadn't envisioned marriage intersecting so abruptly with the momentum I was building. His question landed with a gentle gravity, prompting me to pause and reflect. I asked for time—not out of doubt, but out of respect for the life I was shaping and the dreams I still held close. I needed space to breathe, to weigh the possibilities: the life I was fiercely carving out for myself, and the life we might grow together.

The decision was not simple. I found myself turning over questions late into the night, searching for clarity. Did I want to pause my dreams, or could I carry them with me into a new partnership? Could our ambitions coexist, or would one be asked to bend for the other? I cared deeply for him, and the thought of building a life together held its own appeal—but I was also fiercely protective of the independence and vision that had brought me so far.

After days of contemplation, I finally said yes. It was a quiet, steady affirmation, offered with both hope and a touch of apprehension. In that moment, I recognised that my answer marked a turning point—a leap into the unknown, a willingness to surrender to the possibility of shared destiny.

Such a simple word— "yes"—yet it rippled across every facet of my life. That one syllable altered everything: the trajectory of my dreams, the rhythm of my days, and the meaning I would make from them. It signalled the beginning of a new chapter, one that I sensed would test my resolve and stretch my heart in ways I could not yet imagine. I didn't know what sacrifices might be required, nor how my ambitions would shift and evolve. What I did know was that I was stepping into something sacred—a partnership, a promise, and a path that would entwine my future with another's. The uncertainty was daunting, but it was also filled with hope. I was ready to nurture not just my own dreams, but the possibility of something beautiful we could build together.

That "yes" became the threshold to a new journey—one that would bring its own joys, challenges, and lessons. Over time, I understood that saying yes was not just about accepting a proposal, but about embracing growth, facing change, and stepping into the fullness of life. I was embarking on a partnership that would ask me to share my hopes, adapt my dreams, and discover what it truly meant to intertwine two paths into a single future.

Chapter 14

A Wedding Of My Own Making

When it came time to plan our wedding, I poured myself into every detail. I didn't need to spend big—I had the skills, the vision, and the heart to create something beautiful. I arranged the flowers myself, stitched together bonbonnieres, and designed and printed the invitations. I did my own hair and makeup, crafting a look that felt true to me. My friend offered to make the wedding cake, and together we shaped a celebration that was handmade, heartfelt, and full of meaning.

We honoured tradition with a tea ceremony, paying respects to both sets of parents. It was a grand wedding—over 350 guests. Yet at my table sat only ten people I truly knew, my closest friends. The rest were my parents' guests, my partner's family, and their friends—many of whom I had never met. As I looked around the room, I realised how little I knew about his world. It was a strange feeling, like standing in a crowd and still feeling alone.

In those early days, my understanding of marriage and life was beautifully simple, almost childlike in its naivety, as though I expected a fairy tale to unfold just for me. Every hope I held sparkled with uncomplicated dreams of happiness and harmony.

Before the wedding, I found a house located opposite a park, close to a lake, schools, and shops. It appeared to be a suitable location for raising children. The thought of a home framed by a white picket fence and filled with airy rooms appealed to me, and I envisioned settling there for many years. These choices mirrored what I valued most during that period.

We moved into our new home shortly after the wedding. For a time, everything felt serene and content. There was a sense of happiness in our daily routines, the quiet comfort of shared mornings, the simple joy in furnishing each room, and the peace that came from knowing we had built something together. Our days settled into a gentle rhythm, and with each one, I felt more at home not just in the house, but in the life we were creating side by side.

Looking back, I realise how deeply I believed in tradition, in the reassurance of things unfolding in their proper order: marriage, then a house, then children. Each milestone felt like a stepping stone, a way to fulfil what I thought was expected of me and what, in my heart, I truly valued. It brought a sense of purpose and quiet pride, as though by following this sequence, I was honouring something bigger than myself. It was a period marked by calm, happiness, and a sense of being truly settled.

Soon after, I became pregnant.

Joy and worry appeared at once. The realisation filled me with a rush of happiness, a sense of anticipation for the journey ahead—but also brought moments of uncertainty and concern. As I imagined the future, my thoughts bounced between excitement for new life and apprehension about the challenges that lay ahead.

At sixteen weeks, I sat in the waiting room, counting seconds like prayers.

When they called my name, I followed the nurse into a room where silence pressed in.

The obstetrician placed the Doppler on my belly, her brow tightening. She called for another. Then another.

Three faces, one concern: the heartbeat was slow. Too slow. I waited four weeks for answers that never came.

At twenty weeks, they told me: seventy-four beats per minute. Half of what it should be.

Half a chance.

They spoke of decisions, of outcomes too heavy for hope. I braced for grief—sleepless, raw, unravelling.

But at twenty-two weeks, the monitor sang a different song. The heartbeat had climbed.

They called it a miracle.

I called it a mystery I wasn't ready to trust.

Each week, I returned. For five hours at a time, I remained connected to medical equipment, monitoring rhythms and indications of stability. I expected scientific clarity; instead, I encountered uncertainty. Seeking definitive outcomes, I ultimately faced the realities required for survival.

At thirty-six weeks, everything changed. My body, already weary, began to betray me—preeclampsia surged through my veins, and the medical team decided to induce labour. I laboured for more than twenty-four hours, each minute stretching my endurance and resolve.

I had hoped for a natural delivery. But as the hours passed, something felt wrong. Suddenly, the room shifted—an emergency was unfolding. They rushed me into surgery. Only during the emergency C-section did they discover the umbilical cord had wrapped itself four times around my baby's neck.

She wasn't crying.

There was only silence, frantic hands, and hushed urgency. Time lost meaning. Five minutes felt like an eternity as they worked to revive her. And then—at last—her cry pierced the stillness. Delicate, trembling, but alive. Proof that she was here, fighting.

I didn't get to hold her straight away. The moment she entered the world, she was taken from me before my arms could even reach out, before I could press her tiny body close or whisper her name into the soft down of her hair. Instead, she was whisked across the harshly lit theatre—gently, but urgently—into the care of nurses and doctors whose faces blurred in my memory, all focus converging on the fragile bundle they carried.

I lay on the operating table, heart pounding, eyes darting to catch any glimpse I could get of her. There was no triumphant first cuddle, no warmth of new life gathered into my arms.

Instead, she disappeared into a glass incubator, swaddled not in blankets, but in wires and sensors, monitors blinking in time with her tentative breaths.

The air was thick with antiseptic and anxiety, the hush of the room broken only by the gentle, efficient commands of the medical team.

Through the clear plastic walls, I watched her—so impossibly small, her limbs curled inwards, her chest fluttering with each uncertain breath. Her skin seemed almost translucent beneath the glare, and every instinct in me screamed to hold her, to protect her from the strangeness of this new world. But all I could do was lie there, powerless, separated not only by glass but by fear and the raw ache of hope. We named her Taylor—a name we had whispered to each other in anticipation, but now I pressed my palm against the side of the incubator when finally allowed close, trying to transmit everything I felt—a mother's love, fierce and unyielding—through that cold barrier.

Time seemed to stretch and blur.

Minutes crawled by as I watched the rise and fall of her tiny chest, the gentle ministrations of nurses adjusting her position, checking the monitors, murmuring reassurances I was desperate to believe. I ached to feel the weight of her in my arms, to assure myself she was real, that she had survived, that she was truly mine. The longing gnawed at me, bittersweet and relentless.

When at last I was permitted to touch her, it was with hands scrubbed and trembling, fingertips brushing her impossibly soft skin. She was delicate, but there was a fighting spirit in the way she breathed, in the determined flutter of her eyelids. The doctors told me then that she had been born with a heart murmur, but nothing as serious as what had first been predicted. Relief flooded me—she was, for all her frailty, astonishingly resilient. That first touch—fleeting and gentle—broke me open with a love deeper and more profound than I had ever known. In that moment, every fear, every uncertainty, receded, if only for a heartbeat. All that remained was her, and the overwhelming realisation that I would do anything to keep her safe.

Chapter 15

When The Storm Came

I continued to run my beauty business from home, weaving work around the rhythms of motherhood. Childcare didn't work—my baby kept getting sick—so I kept her close, adjusting my hours, reshaping my days. I was determined to be present, to nurture, to protect.

Meanwhile, my partner was still unhappy in his job. I sat him down, gently but firmly, and asked why he wasn't using his degree to build something better. He listened. He applied. He landed a higher-paying role. For a while, things seemed to shift. He became the breadwinner, and I focused on the home, on raising our daughter, on working part- time to keep my business alive.

The shift was subtle at first.

When we were dating, I never expected him to pay. I was earning more, and I didn't mind shouting dinner or covering the bill. It felt natural—generous, uncomplicated. Money wasn't a point of tension then. We were just two people sharing time, sharing meals, sharing a connection.

But everything changed once we moved in together. Once the children came.

Once he landed a better job.

Suddenly, he became the breadwinner. And with that came

control—not just over income, but over spending, over decisions, over me. I found myself doing things I'd never done before. I started pinning supermarket receipts to the fridge with a magnet, as if to prove my purchases were justified. As if I needed permission to feed my family.

It wasn't just about money.

It was about power.

About how the dynamics shifted quietly, invisibly, until I barely recognised the woman I'd been before.

I used to feel strong. Independent.

But in that season of my life, strength took on a different shape. It became something quieter—less about autonomy, more about endurance. More about surviving the slow erosion of self while still showing up for my children, still holding the thread of love, even when it frayed.

Then I fell pregnant with our second child. And slowly, he began to disappear.

Work commitments multiplied. He had a separate phone—his "work phone". He came home late, often after our daughter was already asleep. Tuesdays were tennis. Saturdays too. Fridays were drinks with colleagues. There was golf. Basketball. Emergency calls at 1:30 am and 2 am. I believed him. I never doubted him. I trusted.

But I was alone.

I gave birth to our second daughter, Ava, and for a while, I clung to hope that we could find a new rhythm as a family. But just before Ava turned two, we received a diagnosis that changed everything: she was autistic. In that moment, the ground beneath me seemed to shift. Suddenly, every aspect of daily life took on new weight and urgency.

I found myself immersed in a world of specialist appointments and therapy sessions, trying to learn the language of support services and advocate for Ava's needs, all while managing the logistics of kinder drop-offs for our older daughter. My days became a blur of driving, paperwork, and phone calls, with barely a moment to breathe between responsibilities. At the same time, my business was demanding more from me than ever, and my own body was growing heavier—I was pregnant again, carrying our third child. The demands piled up, and the loneliness that had been quietly threading through my life only deepened, as I struggled to hold everything together for my children, my work, and myself.

And then came the final blow.

I discovered my husband was having an affair with his ex-girlfriend.

The truth shattered everything. The loneliness I had felt for years suddenly had a name. The silence, the distance, the late nights—it all made sense. And it broke me.

I was pregnant. I was raising two daughters, one with additional needs. I was running a business. And I was alone.

It was too much to bear.

Amid the chaos of motherhood, marriage, and the quiet ache of loneliness, I lost my beloved dog, Kuno. He was growing old, his heart failing, fluid gathering in his lungs. And then, one day, he was gone.

I was heartbroken. I cried for weeks.

Kuno had been more than a pet—he was my comfort, my companion, my silent witness through every storm. He offered a kind of love that asked for nothing in return. Unconditional. Steady. Always there. When life felt too heavy, Kuno would curl beside me, reminding me I wasn't alone.

His absence was unbearable. It felt like losing my best friend. And in the same breath, I lost something else—a precious gift from my father, now gone too. That loss cut deep. It wasn't just an object; it was a thread to my past, a symbol of love and memory.

Everything felt too much. The grief, the pressure, the silence. But even in that darkness, I held onto the truth: Kuno had loved me well. And that love, though quiet now, still lives in me.

Even when the world felt as though it was crumbling around me, I found a way to put one foot in front of the other. Each day, I woke beneath the crushing weight of heartbreak and uncertainty, but somehow, I managed to gather the pieces of myself and keep going. Sometimes it was as simple as drawing a breath, reminding myself that I was still here. There were mornings when even standing felt impossible, yet I forced myself into the rhythm of daily life—making breakfast, packing lunches, shepherding my girls through the routines that tethered us to normality. In the quiet hours between chaos and exhaustion, I would hold my daughters close, feeling their warmth and innocence, and whisper softly to them—and to myself—that love still lived here. Even in the silence, even when hope felt like a distant memory, I tried to infuse our home with gentleness and reassurance, believing that somewhere in those small acts, healing could begin.

Grief and loneliness became familiar companions, shadowing my every step, yet so did a new kind of strength—one I hadn't recognised before. It wasn't the fierce independence I once wore like armour in my younger years; instead, it was a quieter, more enduring resilience. It emerged in the way I navigated each difficult day, not by shutting out my pain, but by allowing myself to feel it and keep moving anyway.

I started to honour the smallest victories: the light in my daughter's eyes when she laughed, the brief moments of peace that surfaced unexpectedly amid the chaos, the comforting memory of Kuno curled beside me, his presence lingering even in absence. Those fragments of joy and remembrance became my lifelines. I let myself grieve openly—some days crying until there was nothing left—yet in that grief, I also made room for hope. Hope that life could eventually offer new beginnings, that pain wouldn't define my existence forever, and that love could find its way back into our lives.

Slowly, almost imperceptibly at first, I began to stitch together a new version of myself—one shaped not only by loss and heartbreak, but softened and strengthened by love. I realised that surviving the storm did not mean being unbreakable or pretending I was invincible.

Instead, it meant giving myself permission to feel everything—the sorrow, the anger, the moments of fleeting joy—and to believe that healing was possible. I learnt that real courage was in embracing vulnerability, letting myself mourn what was lost, and giving space for new dreams to sprout. The journey forward was uncertain, the path often shrouded in doubt, but step by step, I kept moving. In allowing myself to heal, I discovered that I could carry both the ache of the past and the promise of tomorrow, finding meaning and hope woven through even the darkest days.

Chapter 16

The House That Wasn't Ours: A Promise Unravelled

He made promises.

He said he would change. That he would put our children and me first. That he would be a better husband, a present father. He looked afraid when I confronted him about the affair—afraid of losing the life we had built, or perhaps just afraid of losing control.

He convinced me to sell our home. Said we'd move closer to his parents for support, so I could continue my business and have help with the children. I was pregnant with our third daughter. I wanted to believe him. I wanted to give our marriage a chance.

So, I agreed.

I poured my energy into my girls—especially my second daughter, who had just been diagnosed with autism. I didn't understand it then. I treated it like a cold, something that would pass. I was in denial. It was too fresh, too hard to accept. I was still learning how to mother a child with different needs, while carrying another life inside me.

I gave birth to another beautiful girl—Mia.

Her arrival should have been a moment of joy. But what followed revealed the quiet burdens I had been carrying all along.

I'm Still Here

I had married into a deeply traditional Chinese family. Where I came from—a household of four spirited daughters—my husband came from a family of four sons. I was the first daughter-in-law, and when our first child arrived, a daughter, she was cherished and thoroughly spoilt. Her presence softened the household, and for a time, I felt embraced.

When I became pregnant the second time, the doctors monitored me closely due to complications from my first pregnancy. I hadn't planned to find out the baby's sex, but after so many ultrasounds, curiosity got the better of me. Three different doctors told me I was expecting a boy.

So, when my mother-in-law asked, we told her: "It's a boy." She was thrilled—her joy palpable. But when my husband called her after the birth, the news didn't match the expectation. We welcomed another daughter. My mother-in-law was upset, convinced we had played a cruel joke. We explained, gently, that we had simply trusted what the doctors had said. Friends and family had gifted us boy clothes and toys, all in good faith. But the truth was, we had a beautiful baby girl.

During my third pregnancy, my mother-in-law asked again: "What are you having?" This time, I didn't find out. I told her, "They got it wrong last time. I just want a healthy baby." When our third daughter was born, her response stunned me. She said, "You are too weak to give my son a baby boy."

I was speechless. I remembered learning in biology class that the father's chromosomes determine the baby's sex. But I said nothing. I chose silence—not out of agreement, but out of respect. I understood her disappointment, even if I couldn't accept the blame.

But silence has a weight. And over time, it settled into the corners of my life.

When our daughter Ava was diagnosed with autism, the blame came again. This time, it was because I hadn't eaten the right foods. Because it must run in my family. I was already grieving, already overwhelmed. And instead of comfort, I was met with judgement. There was no support. No softness. Just the quiet echo of blame.

I carried the weight alone.

Months later, the house was sold. I packed our things, boxed up memories, and prepared to move in with his parents while we searched for a new home. But then the mail started arriving—letters from the bank, addressed to my husband and his brother. Something felt off.

On settlement day, he took me to the bank. I was asked to sign the cheque. I didn't understand why. But I signed.

He took the money—the entire sale of our home—and placed it into another property. A property under his name and his brother's name. Not ours. Not mine. Not for our family.

He had plotted everything.

He had no intention of rebuilding our marriage. He had no intention of protecting me. He had schemed to protect himself, to secure the assets, to leave me with nothing. All while I was raising our children, managing therapies, running a business, and recovering from birth.

Chapter 17

The Woman Who Held It All: Duty, Silence, and Survival

It was beyond betrayal. It was calculated. Cold. Cruel. I felt numb. The man who promised to love me, to protect me, to build a life with me—had dismantled it piece by piece. I was left standing in the rubble, holding three daughters and a heart that had been shattered.

I was empty. The betrayal had hollowed me out, leaving nothing but numbness and disbelief. In that moment, every part of my life felt stripped away—my trust, my security, my sense of belonging. The man I had counted on, the promises we made, the future we had planned together—all were reduced to ruins. I stood there, holding my daughters close, feeling the weight of loss settle into every corner of my being. There were no words to capture the depth of my heartbreak, no comfort in the aftermath of such calculated cruelty. I was left with nothing but silence and a heart in pieces. Numb from betrayal, hollow from heartbreak.

But even in that darkness, I kept moving. My children needed me, and that was enough to keep me going. I enrolled my second daughter in early childhood intervention, started her in speech therapy, and followed every thread of support I could find. I didn't understand autism fully—not yet. But I was determined to learn, to help, to fight for her.

We moved into the house my husband had bought with his brother, though his brother hadn't contributed a cent. It was just a name on paper. I didn't care anymore. I was too tired to fight. Too broken to resist. I moved in, and then his parents moved in too.

They were kind to me. Gentle. I believed they didn't know what their son had done. I wanted to believe that.

So I became the daughter-in-law they expected. I cooked. I cleaned. I kept the house immaculate. I cared for my children, my husband's parents, and the home. His three brothers came often— bringing girlfriends, staying for dinner. I served everyone. Cleaned up after everyone. Smiled through the exhaustion.

No one asked how I was.

I was drowning in duties, in nappies, in dishes. I was running on fumes, emotionally depleted, physically worn. I was a mess—but a quiet one. The kind that hides behind a tidy home and a full table.

I had become invisible.

But even in that invisibility, I kept showing up. For my daughters. For the elders. For the life I was trying to hold together with trembling hands.

Each day, despite feeling unseen, I continued to fulfil my responsibilities. I rose to care for my children, ensuring their needs were met, and I tended to my husband's parents, maintaining the household and creating order amid chaos. Though my own pain was hidden beneath chores and silence, I persisted—driven by a sense of duty and a determination to provide stability for those who depended on me.

Even as the weight of my circumstances pressed down, I refused to let go. I carried on, not for recognition, but because love and obligation demanded it. My presence, though overlooked, was the thread that held our fragile world together.

I used to think motherhood would be simple.

I imagined love would be enough—that if I gave my heart fully, everything else would fall into place. I never considered the possibility of raising children with disabilities. That reality was so far from my mind; it didn't even exist in my imagination. I was naïve. I thought life would unfold gently, like a storybook: marriage built on mutual love, respect, and understanding; a home filled with laughter and shared dreams.

But life had other plans.

I never expected it to be this hard.

I never imagined how much strength it would take—not just to survive, but to keep showing up with love, even when I felt invisible or overwhelmed. I always believed I was strong. And I was. But the kind of strength I needed… it was different. It wasn't loud or heroic. It was quiet, relentless, and often unseen.

There are days when I still grieve the simplicity I once believed life would hold. And then, almost immediately, a quiet guilt settles in—guilt for even daring to feel this way. I grew up thinking that marriage, a home, and children were the natural sequence of happiness, the milestones that defined a fulfilled life. I told myself that if I followed that order, contentment would follow too. That I should simply accept the life I had built and be grateful, without questioning the parts of myself that still longed for something different, something softer, something more aligned with who I am.

Chapter 18

The Escape: When Silence Turned To Strength

Every morning, I put on my face.

Not for vanity. For survival. For my children. I smiled through the ache, held myself together with trembling hands, and told myself I had to make this work for them. They needed their father. They needed stability. So I stayed. I cooked. I cleaned. I endured.

But inside, I was drowning.

The marriage was loveless. The housework endless. I was invisible, exhausted, and emotionally starved. And then, one day, while clearing out drawers and tossing away rubbish, I found it—a bank slip. On the back, in my husband's handwriting, was a plan. A scheme. A betrayal laid out in steps:

Step 1: Take the wife's name out of the title.

Step 2: Replace the wife's name with the brother's name.

Step 3: Move into the new home.

It was calculated. Cold. Proof that I had been living with a stranger—a man who once seemed gentle, now revealed as a money-hungry monster. The innocence I thought I saw in him was gone. Replaced by greed, manipulation, and cruelty.

I couldn't breathe.

I wanted to scream, to shatter every illusion I had clung to. But instead, I acted.

When he left for work, I packed. My children's clothes. My paperwork. The bare essentials. I loaded everything into the car. I buckled my daughters in, and I drove. I didn't know where I was going—I just knew I had to leave.

We stopped at McDonald's. The girls used the toilet and played on the playground. I watched them, heart pounding, mind racing. Then I kept driving. Further. Away from the lies. Away from the pain. Toward something—anything—that felt like freedom.

It wasn't just an escape. It was a declaration—a line drawn in the sand between the person I was and the person I was determined to become. With every mile that distanced me from my old life, I felt the chains of silence and submission begin to loosen. This act was not born of fear, but of resolve. I was choosing myself, choosing my children, and choosing to reclaim my dignity. No longer would I shrink or contort myself to fit the small and stifling expectations of someone else. Leaving was an act of courage, a refusal to live as a shadow in my own story.

I would no longer be silent. I would no longer be used. I was a mother. A woman. A warrior. And I was done being broken. My pain would no longer be hidden away or explained away for the sake of appearances. Each beat of my heart was a promise to myself: I would speak up, even if my voice trembled; I would fight for what was right, even if I stood alone. My identity was no longer defined by betrayal or by the scars left behind, but by the fierce love I carried for my children and the unwavering strength I was beginning to rediscover within myself.

Chapter 19

The Weight Of Silence: Seeking Shelter, Finding Shame

I drove without a destination, propelled solely by the desperate need to escape. Each mile that slipped by was a silent act of survival, a testament to the storm raging inside me. My children sat quietly in the back seat, blissfully unaware of the turmoil and heartbreak that weighed down every breath I took. I stopped at McDonald's—more for them than for me—giving them a moment to stretch their legs, use the restroom, and play as if everything was normal. Their innocence pierced me. Watching them laugh on the playground while my heart pounded in my chest, I felt both grateful and unbearably fragile. Eventually, I gathered them up and drove on, the road unravelling before me—a thin thread of hope that led away from pain and toward the faint promise of safety. I didn't know where I was going; I only knew that turning back was never an option.

The journey finally ended at my parents' house—a place that should have been a sanctuary. I parked, unbuckled my daughters, and somehow led them inside. The strength I'd summoned to escape dissolved instantly as the front door closed behind me. All the walls I'd constructed to hold back my emotions crumbled. I collapsed, sobbing, unable to speak. For so long, I'd carried the weight of betrayal, sleepless nights, and relentless pretending. I'd shielded my pain from everyone, especially my parents; I never wanted to burden them with the reality of what I'd endured. But in that moment, the exhaustion and sorrow were too much to contain. I could no longer carry it alone.

The relentless stress had hollowed me out, leaving only a shell of the person I once was. I barely recognised myself anymore—physically or emotionally. The weight I'd carried within had, paradoxically, stripped weight from my body. I lost pounds so quickly that I scarcely noticed until others began to comment, their voices laced with concern and curiosity: "How did you lose so much weight after three kids?" But I hadn't tried. The pounds melted away, dragging my self-worth, my dignity, and my very identity with them. My hair started falling out in clumps, collecting in my hands and on my pillow. It was as if I was vanishing piece by piece, a quiet unravelling nobody could see but me.

When I finally found the words to tell my parents I had left my husband, their reaction shattered what little hope I had left for comfort. Instead of open arms and unconditional support, I was met with disappointment and reproach. They couldn't hide their sense of shame and embarrassment. My mother tried to soften the blow, suggesting it was fine to stay for a day or two—no one would suspect anything. But if I remained longer than two weeks, she warned, people would start to notice. There would be talk and judgment, whispers behind our backs. The message was clear: my pain was something to be hidden, my presence an inconvenience, my choices a source of family disgrace.

I'm Still Here

I had turned to my family seeking support, a safe harbour where I could begin to piece myself back together. Instead, I found only shame—a cold reminder that my brokenness was something to be hidden away. Rather than comfort and guidance, their words left me feeling like a failure, the shards of my life swept under a rug of secrecy. The weight of their disappointment pressed down upon me, compounding the loneliness and grief I already carried.

In the end, I was alone once more. Adrift in a house that should have felt like home, yet burdened by isolation as heavy as any I'd known before. But even in that profound loneliness, something inside me refused to surrender. My children needed me, and in time, I realised I needed strength within myself even more.

I clung to the memory of the woman I used to be: strong, creative, and resilient. The woman who once dreamed of opening a florist café, who stitched roses and built beauty from pain. Even as I faded, I held tightly to the hope that I could begin, piece by piece, to remember her. For my children. For myself. For the life I still believed I was meant to reclaim.

Chapter 20

Becoming Someone Else: The Mother Who Refused To Break

I decided to rebuild my life.

Letting go of the pain and disappointment that had defined my recent years became an act of survival. The betrayal I felt—by my husband, by the people who were supposed to stand by me—had left deep scars, but I realised I couldn't let those wounds dictate the rest of my life. The shame, so carefully instilled by whispered judgments and family expectations, no longer served me. Nor did the silence, that heavy cloak I wore to make others comfortable, while I quietly unravelled inside. It was time to turn my attention wholly to the three little faces who needed me most. Amid the chaos and uncertainty, my children became my anchor and my purpose.

Deep down, I knew I had been carrying the weight of responsibility on my own for years—even before I officially left. I was a single mother in spirit, even if not in name, handling every crisis, every bedtime story, every scraped knee and midnight fever alone. The absence of partnership had become my norm, so the reality of being on my own, while daunting, was also oddly familiar. I had already hit rock bottom—emotionally, physically, and spiritually—but in that low place, I discovered a stubborn hope. There was nowhere left to fall. The only direction left was up, toward healing, toward reclaiming my life, and toward building something new for myself and my children. Each day, I resolved to rise a little higher, piece by piece, fuelled by the love I still had to give and the belief that I could be more than what I had lost.

My three girls needed me. And I needed to be strong for them.

We moved in with my parents. I wore my mask each day—smiling, pretending, performing strength. Inside, I was empty. Lonely. But my children pulled me out of bed each morning. Their needs became my rhythm. Their laughter, their tears, their routines—they kept me going.

I had to step away from work. My daughter Ava's behaviour became increasingly difficult. She screamed, head-butted walls and doors, smeared feaces. It was overwhelming. I didn't know what to do, but I kept trying. I enrolled her in services, continued speech therapy, and tried to learn everything I could about her needs.

Yet, leaving behind the work I once loved cut far deeper than I expected. My career had always been more than a paycheck—it was a part of who I was, a source of pride and purpose that gave me an identity outside the walls of my home. Without it, I felt adrift, as though a vital piece of myself was missing. The loss echoed in quiet moments, a subtle ache of incompleteness that lingered no matter how busy my days became.

I poured myself into motherhood, embracing the relentless demands and the fierce love I carried for my children, but even as I gave everything to them, I couldn't escape the sense that I had set aside another version of myself—a woman who had once been seen, valued, and accomplished in her own right.

The role of mother was the hardest, most consuming job I had ever taken, but it sometimes felt invisible, unacknowledged by the world beyond our closed doors. Balancing these feelings—the fulfilment of caring for my daughters and the grief for the self I had left behind—became one of my greatest challenges. I loved my children with all I had, but I quietly mourned the loss of the woman I used to be.

When my parents had guests, I packed my children into the car and drove. To parks, if the weather allowed. To McDonald's, where they could play and use the toilets. I stayed out as long as I could, returning only to put them to bed. I didn't want my parents to have to explain. I didn't want anyone to see.

Chapter 21

Fighting For Fairness: A Mother Against The System

Two years after my separation, my daughters were growing—six-and-a- half, four-and-a-half, and two-and-a-half years old. My second daughter was ready to start kinder. It should have been a milestone. A moment of pride. But instead, it became another battle.

From the beginning, the system failed her.

Before even meeting her, the teacher decided she would attend on reduced hours.

"We'll ease her in," they said.

I believed it was a transition plan. But days turned into weeks. Weeks into months. For four months, my daughter was brought in late and picked up early—her time cut short, her access denied.

She had been approved for a funded teacher aide. It was meant to support her inclusion, her growth, her experience. But she wasn't there long enough to benefit. Her aide was present—yet used for other duties. Helping elsewhere. While my daughter missed out.

It was discrimination dressed as policy. I fought.

I questioned.

I advocated.

But the system was slow, resistant, and wrapped in red tape. I was exhausted, already stretched thin from motherhood, trauma, and rebuilding my life. But I kept going. Because my daughter deserved better.

She deserved to be seen. To be included. To be supported. And I would not let her be invisible.

It took six long months of advocacy, persistence, and quiet frustration before my second daughter, Ava, was finally granted the same kinder hours as the other children. I had fought the system, challenged assumptions, and refused to let her be side-lined. But even as one battle eased, another began.

I started noticing signs in my youngest daughter, Mia—tantrums, sensory sensitivities, and behaviours that echoed her sister's. My heart sank. I knew the path ahead. I began early intervention, sought assessments, and reached out for professional help. I was already stretched thin, but I kept going. Because that's what mothers do.

Chapter 22

The Road Past the Old House: Acceptance And The Weight Of Love

I had left the marriage with nothing but my car and my children. Every dollar I had was poured into the house I bought—only to have it taken, sold, and stripped from me. I received no settlement. I was too tired to fight. Too broken to chase justice. My ex-husband's priority was protecting assets. Mine was protecting my daughters.

I let him win that battle—not because I lacked strength, but because I was utterly depleted. My choice wasn't born of surrender, but of exhaustion. My pride insisted that I could live without the money, that my scarce reserves of energy were better spent on healing myself, nurturing my children, and piecing together the broken fragments of our lives. I reasoned that peace of mind was more valuable than a prolonged legal fight, and I told myself that freedom was worth any financial cost.

Still, word spread through my family and among some friends. They didn't hold back: they called me foolish, reckless, even naïve for walking away from the marriage with nothing. They insisted that no one in their right mind would make such a choice, that I was denying my children what they rightfully deserved. I understood their logic; their criticisms made sense. Perhaps they were right. Looking back, I can see that my decision was impulsive—driven by grief, fatigue, and an overwhelming need to escape. I simply didn't have the strength to fight another battle, especially one waged in courtrooms and through bitter negotiations. At that time, my emotional survival and the well-being of my daughters mattered more to me than any settlement ever could.

I wish I could say I have no regrets, but sometimes the "what ifs" creep in. Even so, I stand by the truth that, in that moment, I did what I could with what I had. And sometimes, simply moving forward—no matter how imperfectly—is an act of courage all its own.

I began searching for rentals in the area. Each time I passed my old house, a wave of grief washed over me. That house had held my dreams—of family, of togetherness, of growing old with love. Now it was just a shell. A monument to betrayal. A memory of what could have been.

Life became heavy.

Being a single mother to three girls was relentless. There were no breaks, no safety nets, no quiet corners to rest. But slowly, I began to accept it. I began to make peace with the idea that I would raise my children alone. That I would be their constant, their anchor, their home.

I didn't want to feel that kind of hurt again. That kind of betrayal. So I chose solitude. Not as a punishment—but as a protection. And in that quiet, I found a strange kind of strength.

I'm not sure whether it was cultural, generational, or simply fear, but in my family—both my parents and my in-laws—there was embarrassment around Ava's disability. They wanted it kept a secret, hidden from relatives and friends, as though silence could erase the reality.

To this day, I don't fully understand it. Perhaps it was shame, perhaps denial, perhaps the hope that if no one knew, the burden would feel lighter. In some cultures, disability is seen as something to be whispered about, something that reflects poorly on the family rather than being understood for what it truly is. But for me, secrecy was impossible. The challenges I faced were too visible, too consuming, too real. Every appointment, every therapy session, every meltdown in public was a reminder that this was not something that could be tucked away.

Keeping Ava's disability a secret felt like denying her existence, her truth, her struggles, and her victories. It felt like denying my own journey as her mother. And so, I carried the tension between their silence and my reality. I felt torn between loyalty to family expectations and loyalty to my daughter's truth.

In time, I realised that secrecy was not protection—it was isolation. It robbed us of support, of understanding, of the chance to educate others and build compassion. It made me feel alone in battles that were already heavy enough. By speaking openly, I found strength. By refusing to hide Ava's truth, I honoured her.

Breaking the silence was not easy. It meant confronting cultural stigma, disappointing expectations, and sometimes facing judgment. But it also meant opening the door to connection. It meant allowing others to see Ava for who she is, not for what they feared. It meant showing that disability is not shame—it is humanity.

Autism is often misunderstood, and with misunderstanding comes judgement. Raising children with autism, I was confronted not only with the daily challenges of their needs but also with the opinions of those who did not understand. People who had never walked in my shoes felt entitled to explain my children's differences, and their words carried weight that was both cruel and dismissive.

Some told me that autism was the result of bad parenting, as if love, patience, and sacrifice could be erased by a label. Others went further, saying it was karma—that in a past life I must have been a bad person, and this was my punishment. Those comments cut deeply. They reduced my daughter's identity to blame and my devotion as a mother to shame.

The hurt was not only personal; it was cultural. In communities where stigma runs deep, difference is often seen as fault. Autism becomes a whisper, a shadow, something to be explained away rather than embraced. I carried the weight of those whispers, even as I tried to shield my children from them.

Yet, in the face of judgment, I learned something vital: ignorance thrives in silence. Every cruel remark reminded me that my role was not only to nurture Ava but also to speak truth against misconceptions. Autism is not punishment. It is not a failure. It is not the result of poor parenting. It is difference—difference that deserves dignity, compassion, and understanding.

I'm Still Here

The journey was exhausting. Each time I heard those words, I felt the sting of isolation. But I also felt a growing determination to challenge the narrative. To show through my children's lives that autism is not a curse but a different way of being. To remind others that behind every label is a child with dreams, fears, and a heart that longs to be accepted.

In time, I came to see these judgments as part of the larger battle. They were not only attacks on me but on the possibility of acceptance itself. And so, I chose to write, to speak, to share our story—not to erase the pain of those comments, but to transform it into a call for understanding.

Chapter 23

What I Gave Away: Debt, Dignity, And The Cost Of Survival

The bills never stopped—school fees, groceries, rent, utilities. With each envelope that arrived, the weight on my shoulders grew heavier. I was already stretched to my limits, both emotionally and physically, but now the mounting financial strain threatened to overwhelm me completely. I had left my parents' house because living there had become unbearable; every time guests visited, I felt compelled to leave, trapped by discomfort in my own home.

I sold everything I could. Jewellery.

Sentimental keepsakes. Pieces of myself.

I had worn my wedding ring and diamond band for years—not out of love, but because they were the last items left from a marriage that had betrayed me. They were constant reminders of pain. I took them to a shop and traded them in. They gave me next to nothing. I brought in necklaces, bracelets—anything I had left. I let it all go.

My children came first.

They needed school supplies, clothes, food, and—most of all—a sense of stability. I was determined to provide, no matter what it cost me. If it meant pawning off sentimental belongings or skipping meals, I would do it without hesitation.

I'm Still Here

There were countless nights I lay awake, stomach empty, but heart heavy with the hope that my children would drift to sleep with full bellies and a small sense of security. Many times, I silently pushed my own hunger aside, quietly offering up my portion at dinner so they could have seconds, or simply enough. Their comfort and well-being became the measure of every sacrifice I made. I learned to survive on less, finding resourcefulness in the face of scarcity, because the thought of my children going without was unbearable. No matter how great the struggle, I would always choose their needs over my own.

Even if it meant erasing the last traces of my past. Eventually, I sold my car.

It was one of the last things I had of value. I used the money to catch up on bills, to keep the lights on, to keep food in my children's tummies. I bought a cheaper car with part of the sale and kept the rest to stay afloat. It wasn't about pride anymore—it was about survival. About keeping a roof over our heads.

And then, things got worse.

I was hit with a debt—over $10,700. I didn't understand. I hadn't bought anything. I hadn't signed anything. But when I asked, they told me it was from a land sale. My ex-husband had purchased land with his brother and sold it for over $2.4 million. He hadn't declared his capital gains tax. And because I was partnered with him at the time, the debt was now mine too.

I had never even known about the land.

85

It was hidden from me—like everything else. I hadn't received a cent from the sale of our house. I hadn't seen a dollar from the land. But there it was: my existence, not my name, tied to the debt. A ghost liability. A trap.

Another secret. Another betrayal. And now, another burden to carry.

I was left to pick up the pieces. Again. Alone. It was so unfair. But I kept going. Because I had no choice. Because my daughters needed me. Because I refused to let his lies define my future.

For so long, I had worn a brave face. I smiled through exhaustion, carried the weight of appointments, sleepless nights, and endless responsibilities. But beneath that mask, cracks began to show.

Leaving the job I loved had stripped away more than financial stability—it had taken a part of my identity. Work had given me purpose, a sense of belonging in the world beyond motherhood. Without it, I felt invisible. I was a full-time carer, yet when people asked what I did, I hesitated. Saying "I'm a carer" felt like admitting to something lesser, even though it was the hardest role I had ever taken on. Maybe it was only in my own mind, but I felt judgment in their eyes. Shame crept in, whispering that I was no longer enough.

The exhaustion magnified those feelings. Ava's ADHD meant nights stretched long past midnight, only for mornings to begin at 4:30. I lived in a haze of fatigue, my body aching, my spirit worn thin. Each day blurred into the next, and I wondered how long I could keep going.

There were moments I broke down in private, moments when the tears came without warning. I asked myself why life had to be so hard, why my children had to suffer, why I had to carry so much alone. The cracks in my armour revealed the truth: I was human, vulnerable, and desperately in need of support I didn't have.

Yet even in those cracks, there was resilience. I kept rising each morning, kept tending to my children, kept fighting for fairness in schools and services. The armour may have been fractured, but it still held. And in those fractures, I began to glimpse something else—the possibility of rediscovering myself, of finding a voice beyond the role of carer.

Chapter 24

A Knock On The Window

By July, my second daughter had finally started kinder with the same hours as the other children. It was a small victory after months of advocacy. My eldest was in grade two, and my youngest was still showing signs that concerned me—tantrums, meltdowns, behaviours that mirrored her sister's. I took her to playgroups, hoping she'd learn from other children her age. I continued early childhood intervention, determined to give her every chance.

Most days, I waited in the car before kinder pick-up, windows down, trying to soothe my youngest through her outbursts. One afternoon, I heard a knock on the window. I looked up—it was one of the dads from kinder. He asked if I needed help. I smiled and said, "No, thank you, I'm fine."

By mid-August, winter had settled in. I waited in the car again, and the same dad approached—standing in the rain, trying to make conversation. I was polite but distant. It felt strange, him standing there, soaked, just to talk to me.

Soon, he began opening doors for me at kinder, making small talk as I left the building. One day, he asked for my phone number. I declined. I wasn't ready. It felt awkward. I was still healing, still protecting myself.

But he was persistent—in a gentle way.

One afternoon, he invited me and my children over for dinner.

"Let the kids hang out," he said. "It's just a catch-up."

I hesitated. But he seemed kind. Present. A decent father. So I accepted. I met his three boys—one with Asperger's and ADHD. He understood my world. My struggles. My silence. He was separated, divorced, with two sons from his first marriage and a third from his second. I didn't ask too many questions. I sensed he carried his own pain. We kept the conversation light, focused on the children.

Within three months, something shifted.

We found a connection.

He made an effort with my daughters—park trips, bike rides, gentle conversations.

He taught my eldest how to ride a bike.

It was the first time in years I felt like a family.

He gave my children what their biological father never did: respect, love, attention, and time.

And then—I fell pregnant.

Things moved faster than I had imagined. He asked for my hand in marriage. He wanted to ask my father's permission to honour our traditions and culture. But I was hesitant. My parents still hadn't accepted the breakdown of my first marriage. I knew they wouldn't accept this new beginning.

Still, something whispered in me:

Maybe this is hope. Maybe this is healing.

Maybe this is the second chance I never thought I'd have.

Chapter 25

The Door That Closed: Truth, Tradition, And Tears

I was scared to tell my dad.

I knew he wouldn't approve. I had been building up the courage for weeks, rehearsing the words, hoping to find the right moment. But before I could speak, he called me. His voice was stern, serious. "Come over," he said. "We need to talk."

My heart sank.

The fear and anxiety were suffocating. I loved my dad deeply—his approval had always been an anchor in my life, a source of stability and pride. Even as an adult, I longed for those rare moments when he would look at me with pride in his eyes, when I felt I had done something that made him happy. Knowing that what I was about to reveal would likely shatter that fragile connection broke me inside. The thought of disappointing him, losing his support, or having him look at me with anything other than love was almost unbearable.

As I walked up to his house, every step felt heavy. My mind raced through old memories—being a little girl and holding his hand, how his approval had shaped my choices, the way he used to encourage me, and how much I wanted to make him proud. This wasn't just about sharing news; it was about risking the bond that meant more to me than words could express.

When I stepped inside, I could feel the tension radiating from him. I had planned to explain everything gently, to give him space to process and maybe, in time, to accept. I clung to a hope that the love between us would carry us through. But I never got the chance.

I went to his house, planning to tell him about my new relationship. I wanted to explain gently, to share the truth on my own terms. But I never got the chance.

When he confronted me, his words were sharp, and his expression closed. I felt like a child again, caught in a storm of disappointment and anger. Every accusation, every demand, cut deeper because it came from someone whose love I'd never doubted and whose acceptance I craved above all. The questions he threw at me weren't just about my choices—they felt like questions about my worth, my loyalty, my place in his heart.

The shame that washed over me in that moment was overwhelming. I wanted to plead for his understanding, to explain that my choices weren't meant to hurt him or betray our traditions. But all I could feel was the sting of rejection. It was as if, in that instant, a wall had gone up between us—a wall made of harsh words, wounded pride, and the heavy weight of expectations I had failed to meet.

Telling him I was pregnant felt like the final blow. Watching his face harden, hearing his voice rise, and hearing him order me out—it was like a door slamming shut on a part of my life I had always cherished. I felt exposed, abandoned, and deeply alone. The pain was not just from his words, but from the realisation that the person I loved so much could cast me out so completely, all because I had chosen a different path than the one he had hoped for me.

As I walked out, tears streaming down my face, I felt an emptiness settle in my chest. The rejection wasn't just about being turned away from his house; it was about being pushed out from the centre of my family, the place where I had always sought comfort and belonging. I grieved not only the loss of his approval, but also the loss of the relationship as I knew it—a relationship built on trust, love, and the hope that no matter what, we would always find our way back to each other.

The aftermath lingered. My partner saw the pain etched in my eyes, the silence that hung between my words. He felt the rejection as well—a widening rift that wasn't just between me and my father, but between him and the family, and between us and the traditions that had shaped my life. The hurt followed me, a shadow that made even moments of hope feel bittersweet. I loved my dad. All I had ever wanted was for him to see me, to accept me, and to believe that I was worthy of love and happiness—even if it didn't look the way he expected.

The pain of that rejection became a part of me, shaping how I moved forward and what I longed for—a second chance, a moment of grace, or simply a glimmer of understanding from the man whose acceptance meant everything to me. Instead, all I faced was a door slammed shut and the harsh command never to return to the place I once called home.

Chapter 26

A New Beginning

Life felt like it was finally settling.

I had a companion—someone kind, caring, and present. My new partner brought warmth into our home, and for the first time in a long while, I felt like I wasn't doing it all alone. The girls were adjusting well. My belly was growing, and so was a quiet sense of hope.

One day, a dear friend called. She was getting married and asked me to be her bridesmaid—and to do her hair and makeup for the big day. I was honoured. It felt good to be seen again, to be trusted with something beautiful.

The wedding was joyful. My girls were with their dad for the weekend, visiting him and their grandparents. After the celebration, I returned home and saw my partner. He asked, half-jokingly, if anyone had tried hitting on me. I laughed, brushing it off. But I told him the truth: the photographer had asked for my number. I didn't give it to him. He left his business card on the bridal table, and I left it there.

But my partner didn't laugh.

His mood shifted. He accused me of taking the number—of hiding something. I was stunned. I told him I hadn't, that I had nothing to hide. But the conversation spiralled. It was our first argument—and I saw a different side of him. A flash of jealousy. A need for control.

I pulled back. I ignored him for two days.

Then he called. Apologised. Said he'd overreacted. That he was just scared of losing me, I wanted to believe him. I told myself maybe this is what love looks like—maybe jealousy means he cares.

Things returned to normal. Or so it seemed.

I left my rental and moved in with him, bringing my three girls with me. We were building a home. My belly grew rounder, and we decided to marry before the baby arrived. We asked my eldest daughter for her blessing; she smiled and said yes. Her approval meant everything to me. He knew that.

We got married. The girls were settled. The house was full of laughter, toys, and the scent of home-cooked meals. For the first time in years, I felt like life was falling into place.

I let myself believe in happiness again.

Silence can be heavy. It can echo with the words you long to hear but never come. For years, I waited for Ava's voice, hoping each therapy session, each intervention, would unlock the sound of her speech. When it didn't, I grieved.

I was doing everything I could. Every week was filled with specialist appointments, speech therapy sessions, and early intervention programs. I kept a calendar that felt more like a lifeline— each appointment a thread I clung to, hoping it would lead us somewhere brighter.

I'm Still Here

By the age of five, Ava was still non-verbal. I tried not to let discouragement take root, but it crept in quietly. I watched other children chatter and play, and I wondered if I would ever hear her voice.

One day, I asked her psychiatrist for the truth I was afraid to face. "Do you think she'll ever talk?" I whispered. He looked at me with compassion and said gently, "In my experience, if a child hasn't started forming words or sentences by age seven, they often remain non-verbal."

That truth landed like a stone in my chest. I nodded, but inside, I was breaking. I had to prepare myself—not for giving up, but for letting go of the version of the future I had imagined.

Still, I didn't stop. I kept going to therapy. I kept showing up. I kept believing that every effort mattered, even if the outcome looked different than I'd hoped.

When Ava turned seven, the weight of that milestone was unbearable. She was still non-verbal. I grieved—not just for the silence, but for the conversations we might never have, the words I longed to hear. I grieved for the birthday wishes she couldn't say, the "I love you" that might never come in speech.

It was hard to accept. But slowly, I did.

And in that acceptance, I began to see something else: Ava was communicating. Not with words, but with gestures, with presence, with intention. She started pointing to things she wanted. She would take my hand and lead me to what she needed. She began using her picture book filled with visual images she used to make requests instead of screaming.

To bridge the silence, I began wearing picture cards on a chain around my neck—simple images for everyday commands and routines: eat, drink, toilet, wash hands. They became a visual language we could both rely on, a way to turn the chaos of unmet needs into something tangible.

These were small steps—but they were monumental. They were her voice, emerging in a language all her own.

I learned to listen differently. To celebrate differently. To understand that communication is not limited to speech—it is connection, it is effort, it is love.

Ava was telling me things all along. I just had to learn how to hear her.

The process was slow and often frustrating. It took time for her to grasp how to use the cards, how to connect the image with the action, and how to ask instead of scream. But each small step forward felt monumental. Every time she reached for a card instead of banging against the wall, I saw a glimmer of progress—a fragile thread of connection between her world and mine.

Chapter 27

Behind Closed Doors: When Love Turned Into Surveillance

Life continued with my new partner. His father lived with us too, quietly tucked away in a caravan in the backyard. He was respectful, kind, and accepting of me and my girls. For a while, it felt like I had found a family again.

But slowly, the cracks began to show.

Whenever we went out in public, I noticed my partner's eyes watching me—closely, tensely. If another man glanced in my direction, even briefly, his mood would shift. His jaw would tighten. His tone would change. I brushed it off at first, telling myself it was just insecurity. But it kept happening.

My second daughter had started attending a special development school. A school bus came to our home each morning to collect her. I always greeted the driver and the assistant with a warm "good morning," grateful for their help. It was simple kindness.

But my partner didn't see it that way.

He accused me of flirting. Of dressing to impress the bus driver. One hot morning, I wore a summer dress—light, comfortable, practical. He exploded. Said I wore it for attention. That I was trying to seduce someone. I was stunned. Hurt. Confused.

Then came the name-calling.

Foul language poured from his mouth—words meant to shame, to belittle, to control. I started to see a different person—someone angry, possessive, volatile. Someone who didn't trust me. Someone who didn't see me.

Even a ten-minute trip to the shops became a battleground. He'd call me while I was out, keep me on the phone, ask where I was, what I was doing, who I saw. I felt watched. Monitored. Controlled.

The house that once felt like a refuge now felt like a cage. I was sad. Alone. Again.

Everything I did seemed to provoke him. Every smile, every outfit, every moment of independence. I was walking on eggshells, shrinking myself to avoid conflict. And yet, the conflict kept coming.

I had survived betrayal before. But this was something else. This was surveillance disguised as love. Possession disguised as protection.

And I was beginning to see it clearly.

Chapter 28

The Shower That Held Me

My son came early.

I was meant to have a fourth caesarean—just like my three girls before him. But at 36 weeks, my body had other plans. Contractions came fast, fierce, and relentless. There wasn't enough time for the hospital to prepare for surgery.

I was terrified.

I felt hands holding me down—arms, legs, shoulders. The doctor kept saying, "Push." I cried out, "This isn't meant to happen." But no one stopped. I felt every cut. No sedation. No anaesthesia. Just pain. Blinding, excruciating pain.

I wanted to die on that table.

I started to haemorrhage, rapidly losing blood. My body wasn't prepared for a natural delivery after three previous C-sections, and the risk was overwhelming. Every moment felt precarious—my history of surgical births meant that my body was not meant to go through labour this way. As the bleeding intensified, fear gripped me even tighter. The medical team worked quickly, but the situation was dire. The reality of my condition set in: I was experiencing a complication that should never have happened, and I was terrified of what might come next.

Time slowed. My body screamed. And then—finally—he was born. A beautiful, healthy baby boy. But I didn't get to see him. I was rushed away, still bleeding, still broken, still needing to be stitched back together.

Much later, I held my son Mason in my arms. The weight of him against my chest was both grounding and surreal. After the chaos and trauma of his arrival, those quiet moments together felt almost surreal.

I studied his tiny features—his perfect skin, the way his fingers curled instinctively around mine. He was perfect. Soft. New. The beginning of something so special, a new chapter unfolding right before me.

Yet, as I cradled this perfect little being, I couldn't ignore the sense of loss that lingered within me. Something inside me had been left behind in that hospital room—a piece of myself I couldn't quite name or recover. The tears came without warning, uncontrollable and raw. I didn't know if it was postnatal depression, if it was the trauma of what I had just survived, or if it was the weight of everything I had been carrying. Maybe it was all of it—grief, pain, exhaustion, and joy, tangled together in ways I couldn't unravel.

I didn't know. I only knew that something had shifted, and I was left searching for who I was, now that he was here.

The hospital recommended I stay longer, but my partner insisted I was ready to go home. My husband discharged me against the doctor's recommendations; I didn't argue. I just accepted. The girls came back from visiting their dad's parents.

I placed my son's cot beside our bed—on my side. Close. Safe.

I thought that with the arrival of our baby, there might be a shift in my marriage. A part of me believed that welcoming a new life into our family would soften the edges of our relationship, bringing us closer together and healing the wounds that had built up over time. I hoped the joy and innocence of a newborn would inspire gentleness, understanding, and maybe even a fresh start for us as partners.

But instead of improving, things continued to deteriorate. The tension lingered, growing heavier with each passing day. The challenges we faced did not fade away with the birth of our child—instead, they seemed to intensify, casting a shadow over the hope I desperately clung to. The promise of change felt further and further out of reach, and I found myself confronting a reality that was even more painful than before.

The jealousy. The mind games. The control. Every time I tried to leave, he threatened suicide. So I stayed. He'd apologise, then start again. My daughter Ava's behaviour escalated. When she struggled, he yelled—at her, at me. I prayed each day that she'd come home from school in a good mood. That maybe we'd have peace. But peace never came.

The verbal abuse became routine.

He made threats towards me and my family, claiming that he would drive his car into my parents' house. The menace in his voice was unmistakable—he wanted me to believe he was capable of anything, even putting innocent lives in danger.

Every time he grew angry, he'd repeat this threat, using it as a weapon to keep me compliant and afraid. I lived in constant terror, imagining the screech of tyres outside my childhood home, wondering if one day he would actually follow through. The fear for my parents' safety became a heavy burden, leaving me on edge and unable to find peace. His words weren't just empty threats; they were a form of control, a way to isolate me and remind me of how powerless I felt under his dominance.

I was punished. Stripped of blankets and pillows, I was forced to sleep on the hard floor—just 50 centimetres between my bed and my son's cot. The cold, unyielding surface offered no comfort, only a constant reminder of how powerless I had become. I curled up in that narrow space, trying to make myself as small as possible, hoping to disappear into the shadows and escape his notice.

Exhausted and desperate for rest, I tried to cover my face with a blanket, searching for even a shred of warmth and solace. But he took it away, leaving me exposed and vulnerable. The simple act of seeking comfort was denied to me, reinforcing my isolation and the control he held over every aspect of my existence.

And then came the worst part.

After each barrage of insults, after the shouting and the humiliation, he would demand intimacy from me. I was left with no choice but to comply, forced into physical closeness with a man who had just shattered my spirit. The very person who had just hurled cruel words and stripped away my sense of worth now expected affection, as if nothing had transpired. Afterward, he would offer an apology—words meant to erase the pain, to pretend that none of it had ever happened.

With every repetition of this cycle, I felt myself fading. Each time, I lost a little more of who I was.

My bathroom became my sanctuary. It was the only space where I could exist without judgment, without fear. I'd sit under the shower, the steady stream of water masking my tears and muffling the sounds of my sobs. The warmth of the water was the closest thing I had to comfort, and I craved its embrace. Each droplet felt like it was trying to wash away the pain, stripping me of my identity, my dignity, my self-worth. I watched as the water swirled down the drain, imagining it was carrying away the pieces of me that no longer fit, the fragments that had been chipped away by cruelty and neglect. I didn't recognise the woman I had become. The reflection staring back at me in the steamed-up mirror was someone faded, her eyes hollow with exhaustion and grief. I was a shadow. A mother holding on for her children. A survivor, desperately searching for traces of herself among the ruins.

But I was still here. No matter how much I wanted to disappear, something kept me anchored. Maybe it was hope, fragile and flickering. Maybe it was the love for my children that refused to die, even when everything else felt lost. Through every night on the cold floor, every harsh word, every moment I struggled to breathe, I found a way to keep going. I clung to the tiniest sparks of resilience, determined to survive—if not for myself, then for those who depended on me. I was battered, but not broken. Somewhere deep inside, the will to endure remained, stubborn and quietly defiant against the darkness that threatened to consume me.

There were countless nights when I questioned myself, wondering why I continued to stay and try to make things work. My husband now was just as cruel, just as unkind as the one before him. Yet, despite the pain, I stayed. The truth was, I felt completely stuck. I carried the heavy weight of shame and embarrassment, knowing I had already disappointed my family once.

The fear of failing again in my second marriage was suffocating. I felt completely paralysed, unable to make a move or speak up for myself. The thought of what others would think haunted me—being seen as someone who had failed not once, but twice, was unbearable. The weight of this shame and the overwhelming pressure not to disappoint anyone again kept me stuck in place. I was so consumed by guilt and the fear of judgment that I convinced myself I had to endure, no matter how much it hurt. Even more, I couldn't bear the idea of my children being without a father again. That possibility was too painful to face, so I stayed, trapped by my own need to protect them and my desperate hope to avoid another loss.

Chapter 29

Trapped Between Two Monsters

I used to be confident. Proud. I don't know when that woman disappeared.

How did I let these two men treat me this way? All I ever gave was love. Honesty. Commitment. They treated me like I was their everything—until they dropped me. Until they let me fall.

After the traumatic birth of my son, Mason, my partner began talking about having more children. I had nearly died. But he didn't care. He measured my love by how many children I had with my ex-husband. "You must have loved him more," he said. And somehow, it was always my fault. My silence was disrespectful. My words were wrong. My existence was the trigger.

He didn't work. He stayed home to monitor me. He had access to everything—my phone, my emails, my social media. I deactivated my accounts just to keep the peace. His mood swung wildly—affectionate one moment, cruel the next. I thought maybe it was bipolar. I begged him to seek help. But he said I had turned him into this monster.

I prayed every day that he would change.

I made excuses. Maybe it was the betrayal from his past. Maybe he was just wounded. Maybe he wasn't always bad. But the rage kept coming. He smashed our photos. Tore my clothes. Threw my belongings outside. Woke the kids in the middle of the night and threw us all out of the house. It happened every few weeks. Like clockwork.

His father never intervened.

I used to wonder why. Why didn't he help us? Why didn't he speak up?

And then I realised—he was just as scared as I was.

I hid myself from the world. Focused on my kids. I felt guilty. All I wanted was a safe, loving life for them. But I had walked into another prison. My ex-husband had controlled me financially. Now I was being controlled emotionally, sexually, and physically. After dropping the kids at school, I'd cry. I didn't know how to escape.

I felt trapped in a maze with no exit.

Then one day, my father-in-law came back from a medical appointment. He looked pale. Quiet. I asked if he was okay. He told me he had prostate cancer. I listened. I comforted him. I cooked for him. I tried to be kind.

But things changed.

He began saying strange things. That I deserved better. That he could love me. That I was the only one who had shown him kindness since his wife died. I told him to stop. That he was confused. That I was his daughter-in-law. He apologised. Asked me not to tell his son.

I promised I wouldn't. But he didn't stop.

He grabbed my hand. Tried to kiss me. Pinched me. And one day, while I was changing my son's nappy, he came up behind me and put his hands down my top.

I felt disgusted. Violated. Humiliated.

I began locking the bedroom door. When my husband came home and couldn't get in, he exploded. Accused me of cheating. Took my phone outside and smashed it with a hammer. "This is what happens when you lock me out!" he said.

I ran.

I walked towards the train station, sobbing. I wanted it all to end. But then I thought of my children. I couldn't leave them. I couldn't abandon them. I turned back.

He was waiting. Cold. Piercing eyes. Swearing. Screaming.

I didn't recognise him anymore.

Was this the man I met? Or had that kind-hearted version of him been a disguise—a lie to lure me in?

I learned early how to carry pain quietly.

There was no space to fall apart in our house. No room for softness, no one to ask how we were really doing. My sisters and I became fluent in silence. We knew how to read the air before we spoke, how to shrink ourselves to avoid conflict, how to soothe each other with whispers and pretend everything was fine. We didn't talk about the things that scared us. We just kept going. That was survival.

But I never wanted that kind of silence for my children.

The moment I held my daughter for the first time, I felt something fierce and protective rise in me. Her tiny body curled against mine, warm and perfect, and I made a vow—not out loud, but in the quiet centre of my being: You will be safe. You will be loved. You will never have to hide your pain. I would give her the childhood I never had. A home filled with gentleness. A mother who listened. A life where she could be her full self, without fear.

I built my life around that promise. Every decision, every sacrifice, every sleepless night was made with her in mind—and later, with all my children in mind. I wanted to be the mother who broke the cycle, who turned pain into protection, who gave her children the kind of love that wraps around you like a warm blanket and says, "You're safe here."

But life had other plans.

Despite all my intentions, all my love, the world found its way in. The kind of suffering I thought I had left behind came back in new forms—quieter, maybe, but no less cruel. My children have known fear. They've felt the weight of things no child should carry. And I've watched, helpless, as pieces of their childhood slipped away.

There are moments that haunt me. Times when I saw the light dim in their eyes. Times when I couldn't protect them, no matter how hard I tried. Times when I felt the old silence creeping back in—not because I taught it to them, but because the world did. And I wonder, *did I fail them? Did I break the promise?*

I'm Still Here

There is a guilt that lives in me now. A quiet ache that whispers, "You promised." And I did. I promised them something better. I wanted to rewrite the story. Instead, I fear I passed down a different kind of ache. But I still believe in the power of love. I still show up. I still hold them when they cry, even if I can't fix what's broken. I still fight for their joy, their healing, their right to be children. Maybe that's what keeping a promise looks like when the world doesn't cooperate—loving them through the storm, even when I can't stop the rain.

Chapter 30

The Night I Ran: The Will To Escape

He had smashed my phone. Then, days later, he gave me one of his old ones. Same number. Same control.

Then came the call.

It was the recreational centre. My mum had collapsed at the pool. I was still listed as her emergency contact from years ago. I hadn't seen her in so long. My dad had disowned me. He hadn't even met my son. But this was an emergency.

My son was asleep in his cot. My girls were at school. My third daughter, Mia, was at an occasional care. I told my husband, "I know you don't like my parents, but I need to go." He didn't reply. Just walked away.

I left anyway.

At the centre, I found my mum in the sick bay. She had taken new medication on an empty stomach. She was okay, just shaken. I held her hand. I called my dad. He came. It was the first time I'd seen him in over eleven months. He looked thinner. Older. I said, "Now that you're here, I'll go."

I drove back to pick up the girls. My second daughter's school bus was due soon. It was Friday—their weekend with their dad. I knew what was waiting for me at home. The silent treatment. I preferred it to the yelling.

It was late. The house was quiet, but the air was heavy, charged with something I couldn't name yet. I knew the tension. I knew the signs. I'd learnt to read the silence like a warning.

But that night, silence turned to violence.

The girls were gone. My son was asleep. It was cold. I was already shaking—part fear, part winter chill. He walked into the kitchen, grabbed an empty 2-litre Coke bottle, and filled it with cold water. I thought he was getting a drink.

He wasn't.

He walked toward me and poured the water over my head. I gasped. He filled it again. I tried to change out of my soaked clothes, but he chased me from room to room, drenching me again and again. He pulled my hair. My neck. I tried to shut the doors, but he forced them open. The whole house was soaked. Even the kids' beds. Their blankets. Their mattresses.

He screamed at me. Called me every name he could think of. "You abandoned me for your bitch of a mother," he spat. "They never accepted me, but you still run to them!"

And then—he spat at me.

Over and over. As he shouted about betrayal, about abandonment, about how I had left him and our son. Spit landed on my face, my clothes, my skin. I felt sick. Humiliated. Dehumanised.

I tried to explain. "They're still my parents. I had to go." He didn't care.

He dragged me by my legs through the house. When he let go, I ran to the bathroom. Tried to lock the door. He forced it open. Grabbed me by the neck. Started choking me. I stopped resisting. I looked into his eyes—cold, empty, evil. I gave up.

And then he let go.

For a moment, I thought he'd come to his senses. But I was wrong.

Then he snapped.

He walked to the kitchen. I heard the drawer open. Heard the clink of metal. He came back holding a knife.

His eyes were cold. His voice was sharp.

"If you don't leave," he said, "I'll stab you in the eye!"

I froze.

Then he shouted, "Get your things. Get the fuck out of here!"

I didn't cry. I didn't scream. I moved. I packed. I grabbed what I could. My heart was pounding, but my mind was clear. I had to get out. I had to protect my children. I had to survive.

That night changed everything.

It wasn't just the threat. It was the clarity. The moment I knew— this is not love. This is a danger. And I will not stay.

This was my chance.

I grabbed a bin bag. Stuffed it with my girls' clothes. Some of mine. I went to get my son. He blocked me. "You're not taking him," he said.

I turned back to the door.

As I hurried to collect our things, my hands trembling but determined, he stalked over to the front door. Without a word, he unzipped his pants and, in a final act of cruelty, urinated all over our belongings. The pungent, acrid smell filled the air, seeping into my clothes, my daughters' clothing, everything we owned.

Each drop seemed fuelled by his rage—his anger soaking our lives, marking my escape with a humiliation I would never forget. My hands shook as I stuffed our now-wet clothes into the bin bag, the fabric heavy and cold in my grip. Even then, I refused to let him break me. This was his last attempt to assert control, to hurt us one final time before we left. But I would not let his hatred stain my will to survive.

I loaded the car. Drove just around the corner. Parked. And cried.

The car reeked of urine, the stench rising from the soaked clothing and belongings crammed into bin bags at my feet. It clung to the air, invading my lungs with every shaky breath. My body ached from being dragged, pursued, and choked—every muscle throbbed with pain from the violence and fear I had just survived. Tears stung my eyes, but I held them back; my heart felt shattered, each beat echoing the trauma of what I had endured. Numbness washed over me, caught somewhere between shock, terror, and the surreal realisation that this was truly my life—this was the point I had dreaded, but knew I had to face.

My hands trembled on the steering wheel as I tried to steady myself, the reality of what had happened settling heavy on my chest. I was exhausted, physically and emotionally, every part of me raw and exposed. The humiliation of what he had done, the cruelty of it, still pressed against my skin, but beneath it all was a small, steady pulse of relief.

For a moment, I just sat there, letting the weight of the night settle around me. The silence inside the car was immense, broken only by the sound of my uneven breathing and the occasional shudder of a sob that escaped. My mind replayed the events over and over—the shouting, the blocking of the doorway, the vile act at the threshold, the desperate rush to gather what I could for my children and myself. I was haunted by the image of his face, twisted in anger, and the knowledge that I had left my son behind, powerless to do anything else.

But I was out. Despite the pain, the shame, and the terror, I had made it through the door. I had escaped. It was not the way I had ever imagined leaving, but I had done what I needed to survive, to protect my children and myself from further harm. There was fear, yes, but also a fragile sense of hope—a trembling belief that maybe, just maybe, this was the first step toward something better. The night had broken me in so many ways, but it had also given me a strange, fierce determination. I was out, and for the first time in a long time, I was free to decide what happened next.

Chapter 31

The Call That Saved Me

I googled Safe Steps—an emergency line for women and children. My hands were shaking. My voice barely worked. When the woman on the other end answered, I tried to speak, but the words wouldn't come. She struggled to understand me. I kept looking over my shoulder. He could've been hiding in the dark, watching.

She gave me an address.

I typed it into my GPS. It was over an hour and a half away. I looked at my fuel tank, praying I had enough to get there. I climbed into the car, alone, terrified, and started driving.

He called me.

I didn't answer. But my thoughts raced: Is my son okay? Is he safe?

I cried as I drove, the tears blurring my vision until the motorway's lines shimmered and split. My hands clung to the wheel, knuckles white, heart hammering, pulse roaring in my ears louder than the engine. I missed turn-offs, doubled back on dark, unfamiliar roads, each mile stretching impossibly long. The sense of being lost pressed in on me with every wrong turn—a gnawing fear that maybe I'd never find safety, that maybe he was still somewhere behind me, hunting in the dark. It took me over two and a half hours to reach the safe spot—a place that felt more like a ghost town than a sanctuary.

It was unfamiliar. Quiet. Empty. Shadows pooled under the streetlights, twisting into shapes I couldn't trust. I had no one. No family. No friends. Just the echo of my own breath and the weight of everything I'd survived. The silence felt perilous, as if it could shatter at any moment.

My phone rang, the sudden sound slicing through the darkness and making my whole body jolt. His name lit up the screen, each vibration a reminder that I wasn't free yet. I stared, paralysed, heart thudding, as if even answering could somehow summon him to my hiding place. He called again. Each missed call a threat, a tether holding me to the fear I was trying to escape.

The phone rang a third time—insistent, relentless. My trembling fingers finally swiped to answer. My voice caught, but I forced it out, steadying myself against the terror. He asked where I was. My mind raced for a plausible lie, desperate to protect myself and, more than anything, my son. "I'm with family," I said, each word shaky but firm. I could almost hear him picturing me somewhere safe—somewhere he couldn't reach. He tried to apologise, his words slippery and loaded, turning the blame onto me, saying I'd upset him because of my parents. His tone veered between soft and sharp. He begged me to come home, weaving promises with threats I knew too well. With every word, my fear deepened, but I kept my answers short and measured, every instinct screaming to keep him calm—for my son's sake.

I forced myself to sound gentle, reassuring. I needed him to believe I was compliant, that I wasn't a threat. My voice was a lifeline, not for me, but for our baby. I kept him calm, my words a shield, even as my thoughts raced through every scenario—what if he found me? What if he went after our child? The fear was suffocating, but I clung to it, channelling it into careful lies and measured responses, all to keep him away, just a little longer.

I waited. Hours slipped by, the night seeming endless. Shadows stretched and shrank with the shifting moonlight, each creak of the building making me flinch. I barely dared to close my eyes. The fear that he'd discover where I was—that he'd take something else from me—kept me alert. Finally, morning came. Light crept across the sky, its arrival both relief and reminder that a new challenge waited. My body felt hollow but determined.

But I wasn't going back alone. I refused to walk through that door without protection, refused to be vulnerable again. The memory of his anger haunted me, sharper now in the daylight. I called the police, my voice steadier this time, the fear now tempered by determination.

I returned with the police—their presence a barrier between me and the nightmare I'd fled. My heart pounded, but for the first time, I wasn't powerless. Every step was heavy with dread and hope, each breath a mix of terror and the faint promise that maybe, just maybe, I was finally safe.

Chapter 32

The Last Chance: When Hope Wasn't Enough

The police questioned me. So did child protective services. I told them everything—every detail, every bruise, every moment of fear. He denied it all. Said I was lying. Said none of it ever happened.

We went to the children's court.

He was given a chance. Anger management. Counselling. Supervised visitation with the children. It was conditional—he'd only be allowed near us if deemed safe. They asked if I wanted to press charges. I said no.

I didn't want revenge. I wanted change.

I believed—truly believed—that maybe this was the turning point. That maybe, with help, he would see what he'd done. That he would become the man I once thought he was. Child protection couldn't understand why I forgave him. Why I let him back in? But I thought the system would force him to change. I thought love could still reach him.

Months passed.

He completed his sessions. Child protection closed the case. He was allowed back into the house—just for a few hours, under supervision. He seemed calmer. He smiled at the kids. Held his son. For a moment, I thought maybe—just maybe—this was real.

But it wasn't.

Once the oversight was gone, he showed his true face. He told me he had only "played their game." That he did it to pacify them. That I was to blame—for calling the police, for exposing him. The monster hadn't changed. He had only hidden.

And I had had enough.

I decided: no more chances. No more waiting. No more hoping. The cycle had gone on long enough—every attempt at forgiveness, every glimmer of trust, had been met not with change, but with deeper wounds. With a clarity forged by pain and exhaustion, I made the hardest choice of my life: I would remove myself and the children from his reach, once and for all. This was not just an act of leaving; it was a declaration that we deserved better, that the pattern of control and fear would not dictate our future. I summoned the courage to ask for a divorce, a word that felt both terrifying and liberating as it passed my lips. It was my first real step toward reclaiming our safety and our lives.

He refused. The answer came swiftly, laced with anger and accusation. The notion of letting me go—of releasing the grip he'd held for so long—was unthinkable to him. Instead of acceptance, he met my request with threats and manipulations, making it clear that he would not make this separation easy.

It wasn't love that kept him clinging to the marriage; it was the need for control. Even in the face of separation, he sought to wield power over me—insisting on dictating terms, refusing to cooperate, and using every tactic at his disposal to keep me tethered. It became clear that his refusal was not about heartbreak or loss, but about maintaining dominance. He thrived on my isolation, my fear, and the silence he had imposed for so long.

But I had already begun to break free.

Chapter 33

A Place Of My Own: Stalking, Harassment, And The Fight For Peace

I moved away.

Leaving behind the life I once knew, I packed our belongings into cardboard boxes—each one filled with memories, some painful, some bittersweet. The decision wasn't easy, but I knew staying wasn't an option. My parents' home, once a refuge, could no longer offer safety; he knew every path I might take. I needed distance, a shield of anonymity to protect myself and my children.

But finding a rental was its own uphill battle. As a carer and no longer employed, I faced scepticism at every turn—application after application was declined by real estate agents who saw only gaps, not circumstances. It was disheartening and exhausting.

Eventually, though, I found a modest rental on a quiet street. The house wasn't much, but it offered something precious: hope. With trembling hands, I signed the lease, my heart pounding with a strange blend of fear and relief. As I unlocked the front door for the first time, I whispered a silent promise to myself—this would be a place for new beginnings.

But he didn't let go.

Freedom, it seemed, would not come easily. Not long after we settled in, I noticed his presence again—subtle at first, almost easy to dismiss as paranoia. But the truth revealed itself in the slow, deliberate drive-bys: his car, crawling past our new address, headlights lingering too long. It was a silent threat, a reminder that distance alone couldn't sever his hold. The phone rang at odd hours, his name flashing across the caller ID. Sometimes he would leave voicemails filled with venom or silence, each one a jab at my hard-won sense of safety. He sent taunting photos—images of unfamiliar women, strangers who became pawns in his twisted game. "They're more beautiful than you," he'd sneer, hoping to ignite jealousy or pain. Every message, every gesture, was designed to provoke, to reclaim a sense of power over me that I was determined to take back.

But this time, his tactics didn't have the same effect.

I refused to play his game. Despite the persistent calls and attempts to provoke me, I did not reply. I did not argue or defend myself. I learned to let the phone ring, to delete the messages unread, to ignore the bait he dangled before me. Each act of silence was a small victory, a step away from the chaos he thrived on. I was exhausted from years of manipulation and control, but I was resolved—my peace was worth protecting, even if it felt fragile. I clung to the quiet, to the slow and steady beats of a new routine, determined not to let him draw me back into his storm. For the first time, I began to reclaim my life, brick by brick, boundary by boundary.

Moving forward was not easy. Each day brought new challenges—nights spent listening for unfamiliar sounds, mornings double-checking the locks. My anxiety lingered, but so did my hope. I found myself constantly on edge, unable to relax even within the walls of my own home. I was too afraid to open the windows, fearing that any vulnerability might invite him back into our lives. Every door was checked and rechecked, sometimes three or four times, before I could try to sleep. Even then, my rest was shallow, my senses alert to every creak or footstep. I avoided sitting near windows and kept the curtains drawn, always aware of the possibility that he might be watching. When I left the house, I glanced over my shoulder, scanning for his car or any sign that he was near. Hypervigilance became my new normal—a constant, exhausting state of readiness that shadowed every moment. Yet, through it all, I clung to the small, stubborn hope that one day, I would feel truly safe again.

I poured myself into rebuilding. My children became my anchor and my focus. We made the little house our own—filling it with laughter, painting walls, building routines. The silence I once dreaded transformed into comfort; no more yelling, no more threats. Just the gentle hush of a home trying to heal. Our space was small, but it was sacred—a place where we could breathe, rest, and begin to rediscover a sense of normalcy.

He kept reaching out, trying every avenue to invade the peace I was building. But each time, I made the conscious choice to respond with silence. I would not allow him to shatter the calm I worked so hard to create.

I came to realise that real peace isn't just the absence of violence or conflict—it's the steady presence of safety, dignity, and self-worth. It's a quiet kind of freedom, rooted in the knowledge that I am deserving of respect and serenity. Each day I chose silence, I reclaimed a little more of myself. I wasn't just surviving anymore; I was learning, day by day, to truly live.

And as the days passed, I began to sense the first glimmers of peace returning—fragile, but real. I was starting to find my way back to myself, step by step, breath by breath.

Chapter 34

A New Kind of Connection: The Spark Of Hope

I was rebuilding again.

Tired. Exhausted. Worn thin from years of drama, heartbreak, and survival. I poured myself into my children—into their healing, their routines, their futures. But somewhere deep inside, I still felt alone. I longed for a companion. Someone to talk to. Someone who saw me.

After leaving my son's father, I reached out to my family again. Slowly, we began to mend what had been broken. It wasn't easy. I still felt the weight of shame—married and separated a second time. I avoided family gatherings, afraid of the judgement in people's eyes. I sensed my parents' quiet embarrassment, even if they never admitted it.

Still, I took each day as it came.

I was a mother first. Always. My eldest daughter was healing too. She had built a close bond with her stepfather, and when he changed, she felt the sting of abandonment. She understood more than I wished she did. I sought counselling for her, and she showed such strength. Despite everything, she thrived at school. I was so proud of her.

Most people would have given up on love after what I'd been through. But I didn't. My experiences had taught me what kind of partner I truly needed—what I would never accept again. I was more cautious now. Less naïve. More protective of my peace.

One day, I had an unexpected conversation with my mum. She mentioned online dating.

It was strange coming from her, someone who had never used social media. I hadn't touched social media in over ten years. After my failed marriages, I had nothing I wanted to share. No holidays. No celebrations. Just survival. And I had been with someone who controlled my every move.

Chapter 35

A Shift In Her Eyes

For a long time, Mum held tightly to her traditional values. She believed in staying, enduring, preserving appearances. To her, love was duty. Marriage represented stability and commitment. And when I entered a new relationship after my first marriage ended, she couldn't accept it.

But something changed after my second marriage broke down.

Maybe it was the time apart—the silence between us that stretched too long. Maybe it was the moment I came to her side at the swimming pools, not as a daughter seeking approval, but as a woman standing in her truth. I saw something shift in her eyes that day. A softening. A quiet surrender.

She didn't say much. But she didn't turn away.

And slowly, I began to believe that maybe—just maybe—she did want her daughter to be happy. That she could see the difference between surviving and truly living. That she understood, in her own way, that new love doesn't erase the old; it simply offers a chance to begin again. And this was perhaps why she raised the topic of online dating.

Her acceptance didn't come with fanfare. It came in small gestures. In silence. In presence. And that was enough.

The idea of online dating felt foreign. I told my mum, "I can't even meet someone in real life, let alone online." But the thought lingered. I was curious. Nervous. Vulnerable. What if they asked about my past? How could I explain it all?

Still, I created an account.

I didn't post a photo. I wanted someone to connect with my words, not my face. By the second day, I was ready to delete the whole thing. Most of the messages were shallow. They wanted photos. I wanted a conversation.

Then—just before I deactivated—it happened. One message stood out.

It was from a man with no profile picture. Just like me.

We started chatting. It was easy. Natural. He was kind. Understanding. For the first time in years, I felt like I was choosing. I laughed. I opened up. I hadn't spoken to a man like that in so long.

Eventually, we exchanged numbers. I was nervous to hear his voice. But when I did—it was warm. Gentle. Familiar. Just like his messages.

I told him about my past. My pain. My children. And he didn't flinch. He listened. He shared his own hardships. We clicked.

And for the first time in a long time, things felt... right.

Chapter 36

The Beginning Of Something New

We talked for hours.

His voice was warm, steady, and kind. There was no pressure. No judgement. Just two people sharing stories—two people who had known pain and were learning how to speak again. I told him about my past, my children, my fears. He listened. He understood. He shared his own journey, and I saw the cracks in his armour too.

It felt safe.

For the first time in years, I wasn't being watched, controlled, or silenced. I was being heard. I laughed—really laughed. I hadn't done that in so long. I felt like I was choosing this connection, not falling into it. I wasn't desperate. I wasn't naïve. I was cautious, but open.

There were no games. No demands. Just messages, calls, and the slow unfolding of trust. I told him I hadn't used social media in over a decade. That I'd been in relationships where I couldn't even post a photo or speak freely. He didn't flinch. He didn't ask for pictures.

He asked about my day. My dreams. My children. It was strange and beautiful.

I had spent so long surviving that I forgot what it felt like to be curious about someone. To feel seen. To feel chosen. And this time, I wasn't trying to fix anyone. I wasn't trying to prove my worth. I was simply being myself—and that was enough.

I didn't know where it would lead.

But I knew this: I was healing. I was growing. I was learning to trust again—not just someone else, but myself.

And that was everything.

Chapter 37

Coffee, Pizza, And Just Us: A Gentle First Meeting

I felt safe enough to meet him.

It was a kind of safety I barely recognised—a gentle warmth in my chest, not the tense hypervigilance I'd grown used to. I realised I wasn't looking for escape routes or excuses. I wasn't rehearsing apologies or bracing for disappointment. This was different. The fear that usually clung to me was quiet, almost gone, replaced by cautious hopefulness that maybe, just maybe, this could be something real.

After everything I'd been through, that feeling alone was extraordinary. There was no pressure. No expectations. Just a quiet curiosity and a sense of ease that had been building between us.

We both understood, in unspoken ways, what it meant to be careful with a heart. I could sense his respect for my boundaries—not just in words, but in the gentle rhythm of our conversations, in the way he listened more than he spoke, and in the honest way he shared small pieces of himself. There were no grand declarations, only the honest unfolding of two people discovering each other at their own pace.

We agreed on something simple—coffee and pizza. Nothing fancy. No candlelit dinners or grand gestures. Just two people, face to face, being exactly who we were.

I'm Still Here

I didn't get overly dressed up. Just casual jeans, a black top, and a jacket. Comfortable. Me. He showed up the same way—no pretence, no performance. Just a man in jeans and a jacket, standing tall and calm, like he belonged in the moment.

As I glanced at my reflection in the car window before heading inside, I realised—for the first time in ages—I didn't feel like I had to hide or make myself smaller. Just as I was, I felt worthy—no disguises, no apologies.

And when I saw him waiting, I could tell he felt the same. There was an ease in the way he stood, hands in his pockets, scanning the pavement with a soft, hopeful smile.

When I stepped out of my car, I saw him across the lot—a tall silhouette against the fading light. My first thought was, "Wow, he's so tall." He didn't move right away, just waited with a quiet stillness that felt respectful, not imposing. And then he walked toward me.

My heart was pounding, but not from fear—more like anticipation.

The sun was sinking beneath the horizon, casting everything in a soft, golden glow. In that moment, I felt truly noticed—not as some object, but as someone with a story, with depth, and with dreams.

He matched my pace as I crossed, and for a moment, the noise of the world faded, leaving only the soft crunch of gravel under our shoes and a gentle sense of possibility.

As he came closer, the silhouette softened into a man with a kind, gentle smile. Not the kind that tries too hard—just genuine. Open. Like he was glad to be there, and glad to see me.

I could see the sincerity in his eyes, a sort of vulnerability that mirrored my own. He didn't reach for a hug too soon or fill the silence with nervous chatter. Instead, he offered a simple hello and waited, letting the moment breathe. It was a relief to be met with such authenticity. There were no walls, no games. Just two people, meeting in the middle.

I was nervous, but also quietly excited. There was something about him—a kind of familiarity that lingered at the edge of recognition. It felt almost as if we'd crossed paths before, in another time or another life. Our lives seemed to have been moving along separate tracks, slowly and inevitably converging on this very moment. It was an odd sensation, almost like an invisible force was nudging me forward, encouraging me to meet him. I can't quite put it into words, but it felt like we were meant to find each other, as if destiny had been working behind the scenes to bring us together.

The conversation came easily, as though we were picking up threads from a story already begun. It was strange and comforting at the same time, the sense that maybe fate had been quietly weaving us together all along. I caught myself watching the way his eyes lit up when he laughed, the way he listened intently, never rushing or interrupting.

We talked. Laughed. Shared slices of pizza and stories that had shaped us. There were no masks. No performances. Just honesty. And that was enough.

The conversation drifted from childhood memories to favourite movies, from small heartbreaks to big dreams. There was a rhythm to it, the easy give and take of two people learning each other's edges and soft spots. We joked about things, but didn't shy away from the harder stories. We talked about survival, about resilience, about the scars that made us who we were.

We both walked through fire. Faced heartbreak. Carried burdens that left invisible scars. And maybe that's why it felt so easy— because we understood each other without needing to explain.

There was a silent agreement between us that our pasts didn't need to be hidden, but didn't have to define us either. We honoured each other's stories, recognising the courage it took just to show up. Sometimes we sat in comfortable silence, letting understanding fill the spaces words couldn't reach. It was as if the weight we carried made the table between us feel lighter.

I didn't feel like I had to prove anything. I didn't feel judged. I didn't feel small. I felt… seen.

Maybe for the first time ever, I felt what it was like to occupy space freely, to exist without apology. He didn't flinch at my honesty, and I didn't shrink from his. There was no sense of trying to fix or rescue one another—just acceptance and gentle curiosity, a willingness to witness each other as we truly were.

For the first time in a long time, I wasn't surviving a moment—I was living in it.

When he smiled, his eyes sparkled with a brilliance reminiscent of green jade—one of my most cherished stones. There was a gentle kindness in them, a radiant warmth that seemed to reach out and envelop me, making everything else fade away.

The laughter, the shared stories, the simple act of being present—it all felt like a promise to myself that joy was possible again. Healing wasn't just some distant destination. It was here, right now, in the warmth of a casual evening, in a shared meal, in the honest connection of two people daring to hope again.

And it was good.

Chapter 38

Two Worlds: New Light, Old Shadows

It was new. It was exciting. Each moment felt like uncharted territory, as if I was rediscovering parts of myself I had long forgotten. There was a gentle thrill in the uncertainty—a quiet hopefulness that made even the simplest things feel meaningful. I noticed how my heart would race with anticipation whenever my phone buzzed, each message a small spark of joy. It was as though, after years of walking in darkness, I was finally stepping into dawn, unsure of what lay ahead but grateful simply to feel warmth on my skin.

I looked forward to hearing from him each day—his voice, his stories, the gentle rhythm of connection. It was simple, but it meant everything. After years of silence and surveillance, this felt like sunlight breaking through. The anticipation of a new message or call became a lifeline, an affirmation that I was seen and valued. The way he listened, the way he remembered the small details—these were gifts that reminded me how deeply I had craved genuine connection. His laughter was a balm to the places inside me that had grown sore from mistrust and fear.

We talked about our days. Our thoughts. Our dreams. There was no pressure, no control—just curiosity and care. Things were going so well. Our conversations wandered freely, untethered by the fear of judgment or repercussion. We shared hopes for the future, confided secret worries, and celebrated the small victories that made up our everyday lives. For the first time, I realised how rare it was to be met with real interest, how healing it could be to simply exist as myself and be enough. In those moments, I allowed myself to believe in good things—maybe even a good life.

But the past hadn't let go. Its shadow crept along the edges of my new happiness, casting doubt and unease. Just when I started to trust in possibility, reminders of old wounds would resurface, uninvited and relentless. I tried to shield my new world from the lingering darkness, but sometimes it seeped in anyway, colouring the edges of my joy with apprehension.

My ex continued his harassment. Threats were made towards me and my family. The drive-bys started again—slow, deliberate, watching. If he saw a car in my driveway, he'd accuse me of having a man in the house. Even if it was my sister's car, he'd lash out. He'd never seen her car before, so he didn't know. But that didn't stop him. His presence was a constant reminder that freedom could be fragile, that some battles didn't end simply because you walked away. The anxiety lurked, making me second-guess moments of joy, as if happiness itself was something dangerous to reach for.

He called me names. Sent messages. Stirred up chaos. The harassment was relentless, designed to make me doubt the progress I'd made, to pull me back into fear and self-doubt. But each insult and every cruel message became proof of how much distance I had put between my present and his grasp. Where once I would have cowered, now I stood tall, refusing to let his words define me anymore.

But this time, I didn't crumble. Each confrontation became an opportunity to reinforce my boundaries, to practice courage, and to remind myself of my own resilience. I learned to separate his anger from my worth, refusing to let his bitterness poison the life I was building. I became my own protector, steady and unyielding.

I remembered who I was. I remembered what I'd survived. And I was just glad—so glad—that I had left that relationship. Each memory of hardship was a badge of survival, a testament to the strength it took to leave. Gratitude filled me—not just for the distance from the pain, but for the discovery of new possibilities, new happiness. I was determined to no longer let fear rule my days or dictate my happiness.

That I was no longer under his roof, no longer under his control. I was building something new. With every small step, I reclaimed parts of my life—my laughter, my trust, my hope for the future. The space I inhabited felt brighter, filled with possibility rather than fear. I began to envision a life where my choices were my own, where love and kindness could flourish without threat or suspicion.

And even though the shadows still lingered, I was walking towards the light. Every day, I took another step away from the past and toward the future I deserved. The echoes of pain might never vanish, but they no longer defined me. Instead, with each sunrise, I let hope guide me forward—toward healing, toward joy, toward a life fully lived on my own terms.

Chapter 39

The Road To Safety: A New Beginning

Things were finally going well.

The kids were thriving. I was smiling—really smiling. No more pretending. No more faking joy for their sake. I'd sing in the car, music loud, windows down, heart light. My eldest daughter would tease me, "Mum, you have a weird, funny smile." And I'd laugh, because it was true. It was the smile of love. Of happiness. Of freedom.

But the past hadn't let go.

One day, I was driving with my partner and the kids. We were on a quiet road when my ex appeared—following us. Behind him, another car. His mate. We were trapped. A dead end. Two cars blocked us in. The kids screamed. I panicked. My heart raced.

He stared us down. Cold. Unhinged. His friend watched from the second car.

I grabbed my phone. Called the police. He saw me dialling. Saw the dash cam recording. And then—he backed out. So did his friend.

We drove straight to the police station.

I filed an intervention order. It was granted. The process was long, exhausting, but I got there. He tried to fight back and applied for custody of our son. But the courts saw through it. His case failed.

I'm Still Here

And through it all, my partner stood by me.

He helped submit affidavits. Sat beside me in court. Held my hand through the fear and the flashbacks. He didn't run when things got hard. He stayed. He protected. He listened.

I had to return to court and face not only the legal system, but also my ex-husband—someone whose presence still triggers layers of fear and trauma. Before my matter was even heard, I was taken into a small room to speak with a domestic-violence support worker. She was gentle, but the questions she needed to ask were deeply personal, touching on experiences I had spent years trying to survive.

As I tried to answer, my body reacted before my mind could catch up. My heart started racing, my chest tightened, and my breathing became shallow. The room felt smaller, the air heavier.

I could feel myself slipping into panic, unable to steady my thoughts or my breath. The palpitations became so severe that an ambulance was called. I was taken from the courthouse to the hospital, hooked up to an ECG and heart monitors, while the medical team worked to stabilise me.

It wasn't "just nerves." It was a complete anxiety attack brought on by trauma, by fear, and by being forced back into an environment that my body no longer felt safe in.

Through all of it, my partner stayed right beside me. He saw the fear, the overwhelm, the way my body shut down under the weight of everything I'd been holding. His presence—steady, calm, and protective—made the aftermath a little less frightening. Knowing he was there gave me something solid to hold onto when everything else felt like it was collapsing.

After that incident, I was connected with counselling services, including an organisation that supports people who have experienced sexual assault. Through those conversations, I learned something I had never allowed myself to name: what happened to me in my marriage was sexual assault.

For so long, I believed that because we were married, I had no right to call it that. But I was told—clearly and compassionately— that consent is still required in a marriage. If something happens against your will, it is still rape, even if the person is your husband. Realising that truth was confronting, but it finally gave language to the pain and confusion I had carried in silence for years.

When the court scheduled the next appearance, we chose to attend through Webex from the safety of our home. The difference was immediate. Instead of sitting in a cold courthouse surrounded by tension and memories, I was in my own space, with my partner nearby, able to breathe without feeling trapped or watched.

The process was still stressful, but it was manageable. I could speak. I could think. I could participate without my body going into survival mode. Attending remotely gave me back a sense of control that had been stripped away the first time. It reminded me that healing isn't about pretending the trauma never happened—it's about finding safer ways to move through the things you cannot avoid.

The counselling was extensive and, at times, incredibly confronting. There were moments when the questions felt too heavy, too raw, and I found myself trying to avoid them because saying certain truths out loud felt impossible. Some memories were easier to carry in silence than to speak into the room.

That's when I turned to art therapy. Instead of forcing myself to talk, I painted what I felt. Colours, shapes, and textures became my voice when words refused to come. It was gentler, safer. Through the brushstrokes, I could express things I wasn't ready to articulate.

It reminded me of my childhood—those early years when drawing and writing were my first languages, long before I learned how to explain myself to adults who didn't always listen. Art therapy brought me back to that place where expression didn't require justification. I could simply put my feelings on paper and let them exist without having to defend them.

In many ways, it helped me reconnect with parts of myself I had buried. It allowed me to process the trauma at a pace my body could handle, without being pushed beyond what felt safe.

Healing from trauma wasn't simple or quick. It took time, patience, and a kind of strength I didn't even realise I had. And even now, it's not something that just disappears. The memories still surface, especially in my sleep. There are nights when I wake up drenched in sweat, my heart racing, my body bracing for danger that isn't there anymore. It takes a moment to ground myself, to look around and remember that I'm safe, that I'm far away from what happened, that I'm not living in that reality anymore.

Certain sounds still make me flinch. Sudden movements or footsteps behind me can send a jolt through my body. Sometimes I still scan my surroundings, checking over my shoulder, making sure I'm not being followed. These reactions aren't choices—they're echoes of what I survived.

But with time, the intensity has softened. The fear doesn't control me the way it once did. I've learned to breathe through the moments that used to overwhelm me. I've learned to recognise what is a memory and what is the present.

I'm still cautious, and maybe I always will be. But that caution no longer feels like fear—it feels like awareness, like wisdom earned through experience. And even with the lingering shadows, I can see how far I've come.

My new partner made time for my children.

Took them out for ice cream. For dessert. For quiet moments of connection. He got to know each of them—not just as kids, but as people. He listened to their stories. Their fears. Their dreams.

It felt like fate.

I was never superstitious. But the timing, the way he entered our lives—it felt meant to be. Like he was sent to us. Not to fix us, but to walk beside us.

I began the process of getting support for my son—assessments for autism and ADHD. It was long, complex, and emotional. But this time, I wasn't alone. I had someone who stood beside me. Who didn't flinch. Who didn't leave?

We were safe.

And for the first time in a long time, we were free.

For many years, I carried the weight of this journey alone. Every appointment, every sleepless night, every crisis fell on my shoulders. I was the anchor, the advocate, the carer, the mother—and though I rose each day to meet the demands, the loneliness was heavy.

Then, I found someone who chose to stand beside me. His love was not loud or dramatic, but steady and unwavering. He became the shoulder I could cry on, the calm in the storm, the kindness that reminded me I didn't have to do this alone. His presence gave me courage, his support gave me strength, and his love reminded me that even in hardship, life could hold tenderness.

It was during this time that Ava's health grew more complicated. She began having seizures, each one terrifying, each one pulling us back into hospital corridors and specialist appointments. The diagnosis that followed was devastating: a brain malformation, her brain deviating into her spinal canal. With it came vomiting, migraines, dizziness, and incontinence—an ongoing battle that continues to this day.

The nights become endless cycles of anxiety. Sleep is elusive, replaced by a hyper-alertness that never truly fades. You lie awake, listening for any sign—a change in breathing, a sudden movement—knowing that at any moment, another seizure could begin. The uncertainty is relentless; you cannot plan, cannot rest, cannot escape the constant dread that the next crisis is always just moments away.

This helplessness is not just physical, but deeply emotional. You want to comfort your child, to take away their pain, but all you can do is hold them, keep them safe, and wait. The waiting itself becomes a kind of suffering— a test of endurance and love. Over time, the exhaustion accumulates, leaving you isolated and worn thin.

Yet, even in these darkest hours, when I felt things were too much to bear, I finally had a shoulder to cry on. For so long, I had shouldered the burdens alone—juggling Ava's complex needs, the endless stream of medical appointments, and the constant vigilance that left me physically and emotionally drained. Each night was a battle with anxiety, every moment shadowed by the fear of what might come next. But when he entered my life, everything shifted. His presence was gentle but steadfast, a quiet reassurance in the midst of chaos. I could let my guard down, if only for a moment, and allow myself to be vulnerable. He listened without judgement, comforted me without words, and held me when the tears came. In those moments, I realised I didn't have to be endlessly strong or carry the weight by myself. Having someone truly there for me—someone willing to share the pain and uncertainty—became a lifeline, reminding me that even in the hardest times, love and support could offer solace and hope.

The challenges did not lessen, but the journey became less lonely. Together, we faced the hospital visits, the sleepless nights, and the uncertainty of what lay ahead. His unwavering love became part of my ongoing reminder that strength is not only found in solitude but also in partnership.

Legacy, I have learned, is not only about survival—it is about love. The love I pour into my children, the love that sustains me through caregiving, and the love that now surrounds me in partnership. This legacy is not perfect, but it is real. It is built on resilience, on devotion, and on the courage to keep going even when the battles never end.

I want my children to know that love can carry them through storms. That even when life feels unbearable, there can be moments of grace. That strength is not the absence of struggle, but the presence of love that refuses to let go.

This is the legacy I leave: a legacy of love.

For years, my identity had been swallowed by the role of carer. My days revolved around appointments, sleepless nights, and the rhythm of my children's needs. I had lost the woman I once knew— the one who worked, who laughed freely, who dreamed without limits. But slowly, through small acts of devotion to myself, I began to rediscover her.

Writing was the first doorway. At night, when exhaustion pressed heavy on my body, I would reach for a pen. Words spilled onto the page—fragments of memory, poems shaped by pain, reflections on motherhood and survival. Each line reminded me that I was more than the labels placed upon me. I was a woman with a voice.

Music followed. Songs became a way to release emotions too heavy to carry in silence. I wrote lyrics about betrayal, resilience, and hope. Sometimes the endings were unresolved, reflecting the truths I was still processing. But even unfinished, they carried my heart.

Art and nature gave me sanctuary. Bonsai had already taught me patience and presence, but tending to plants, walking among trees, and breathing in their quiet strength reminded me that growth was possible—even in brokenness.

I began to see that rediscovery was not about returning to who I had been before. It was about becoming someone new—someone shaped by hardship, yet softened by love. Someone who could honour both the darkness and the light.

There were still moments of shame, moments when I felt invisible or judged. But alongside them grew a quiet pride. I was raising four children, caring for Ava, and finding ways to keep my spirit alive. That was not weakness—it was strength.

Rediscovering myself was not a single act, but a series of small, intentional choices: to pick up the pen and write my truth, to sing the emotions I could no longer carry in silence, to nurture both plants and my own weary soul, to allow myself moments of gentle breathing amid the chaos. Each decision, though small on its own, worked quietly to mend the parts of me that had unravelled. Over time, I began to see myself clearly again—not just as a caregiver, but as a vibrant woman with her own dreams, passions, and the hope of creating something meaningful for those who follow. What I built was not just survival, but a life shaped by love, purpose, and the courage to begin anew.

Chapter 40

Full Circle: A Life Reclaimed

I have weathered countless storms that tried with all their force to silence my spirit, to diminish the light within me, and to convince me that I was powerless against the tempests of life. Each challenge threatened to erase my voice, yet I pressed onward, clinging to hope in the darkest nights.

I have felt the crushing weight of betrayal—trusted hands turning cold, words meant to comfort instead wounding deeply. I have endured the sting of being controlled, of having my autonomy stripped away until I questioned my own reality.

The ache of being unseen became a constant companion, an invisible cloak I draped over myself even in the midst of a crowd. I have walked through the fires of adversity time and again, each ordeal leaving me singed but never defeated. Through the smoke and chaos, I pressed onward, carrying my children with unwavering resolve, determined to shield them even as my own heart was breaking. I have been bruised by cruel words and broken by shattered promises, buried beneath the wreckage of relationships that once spoke of love, but ultimately brought only fear and uncertainty.

Still, I rose.

My rising was not immediate, nor was it without pain or lasting scars. Healing came slowly—fragment by fragment, breath by breath—as I pieced myself together with a tenderness I once reserved only for others. In the aftermath of chaos, I sought out safety and nurtured connections that offered true support. I found the courage to set boundaries, to say, "No more," and to reclaim what had been lost or surrendered. It was in those quiet, vulnerable moments—after the storms had passed and the dust had settled—that I discovered something even more profound than survival: I found myself. Stronger, wiser, and unafraid to finally honour the woman I am becoming.

I am no longer the woman who hides behind a forced smile. I am the mother who sings in the car, who laughs with her children, who dares to love again—not because she needs saving, but because she knows her worth.

And in that love, I found more than a partner—I found a family.

His parents welcomed me with warmth and grace. His mother became a quiet anchor in my healing, someone I could talk to for hours, laugh with, cry with, and feel safe beside. His father, too, radiated kindness. Together, they raised a beautiful man—a true gentleman—and for that, I am deeply grateful.

I've learned that healing isn't about forgetting. It's about remembering who you are beneath the pain. It's about choosing peace over chaos, truth over silence, and love that uplifts over love that controls.

Today, I live with intention. I write with purpose. I create with heart. My story is no longer a secret—it's a legacy. One stitched from sorrow and strength, from lullabies and late-night tears, from the fierce, unshakeable love of a mother who refused to disappear.

Through many years shaped by struggle and hardship, I have learnt that leaving and walking away is an act of strength, not failure.

That empathy does not mean accepting harm or carrying pain that was never mine to hold.

That grief is not a weakness but a teacher, revealing what mattered and what must be released.

That choosing peace over chaos is a declaration of self-worth, not surrender.

I have learnt that my experiences are not something to hide.

They are knowledge earned the hard way—proof of my resilience, my clarity, my growth.

They have taught me that I am deserving of love, of happiness, of safety, and that I can choose all three without apology, without hesitation, and without shrinking myself ever again.

I am here. Whole. Awake. Unafraid.

And if even one person reads these words and feels less alone— if they glimpse their own reflection in these pages and dare to believe in their own becoming—then every scar, every silence, every step has been worth it.

This is not the end.

I'm Still Here

This is the beginning of everything. A life reclaimed.

A voice restored.

A legacy blooming—petal by petal, page by page. This life is reclaimed.

Lan Anh Nguyen

Epilogue

Echoes Of The Rain

I once feared the rain—its suddenness, its weight, the way it blurred
the world,

and pressed everything dangerously close to breaking.

But now,

I hear it differently.

It no longer drowns me. Now the rain sings—soft against the
windows, gentle on the roof—reminding me,

that even the sky must let go of what it holds. I have learned to do
the same.

I have wept quietly, screamed into dreams, whispered truths

into empty rooms,

and watched them blossom.

I have let go of names that never truly knew me, and I hold close the
ones who saw me whole.

I have mended myself—with lullabies and lyrics, with poems and
prayers,

with the love of my children, and the embrace of the one who never
left.

So let the rain come.

I'm Still Here

Let it echo. Let it cleanse.

I am not afraid. I am not broken.

I have not disappeared.

I am still here.

And I always will be.

Lan Anh Nguyen

Navigating Parenthood and Embracing Resilience

Motherhood has been both a profound teacher and a continual source of growth for me. Through my children, I have learned lessons about strength, compassion, and perseverance—lessons that have reshaped my understanding of love and endurance.

My second daughter, now 17 and a half, lives with Autism. She remains non-verbal and has also been diagnosed with a brain malformation that causes seizures. Her journey is ongoing, and her needs are constant. In caring for her, I have discovered new ways of listening and connecting—ways that do not rely on words but on presence, patience, and trust. Her silence has taught me to hear differently, and her vulnerability has revealed to me the depth of resilience that exists in both of us.

Parenthood has required me to become an advocate as well as a nurturer. I have had to navigate systems, seek out resources, and fight for her dignity, all while holding space for the tenderness of everyday life. There are moments of exhaustion and fear, yet there are also moments of profound grace—when her smile, her quiet strength, or the simple rhythm of our shared routines remind me that beauty can exist even in struggle.

This chapter of my life is still unfolding. The responsibilities and challenges I face as a parent remain ever-present, shaping not only the lives of my children but also my own path forward. In walking beside them, I have learned that resilience is not about ease or certainty, but about rising each day with love as my compass and hope as my guide.

Dedication

Gratitude and Acknowledgements

My Children: The Guiding Lights

There are those whose steadfast presence anchored me when the world felt silent and overwhelming. Among them, my children shine as guiding lights and the very reasons I continue to rise each day. Their love and unwavering support have been my salvation, offering me purpose and reminding me why I choose hope over despair.

My Partner's Mother: Compassion and Friendship

To my new partner's mother, I am deeply grateful for the patience and understanding she showed as I poured out my pain and sorrow. She stood by me through laughter and tears, her compassion gently softening the aches and cracks in my heart. Her guidance, ongoing friendship, and support have proven that even in the hardest moments, love can be a comfort.

My Partner's Father: Quiet Strength

My new partner's father offered a quiet strength that served as a steady foundation. Through his example, he shaped a man with a gentle soul, someone capable of loving me wholly and without reservation. I am thankful to him for raising such a person.

My Partner: Embracing Renewal

To the man who looked beyond my brokenness and saw the

possibility of growth and renewal, I am grateful for his willingness to weather life's storms with me. His choice to welcome my children as his own has been a gift beyond measure.

Enduring Support: The Roots of Healing

To everyone who stood by me, refusing to flinch or run when faced with adversity, you have become the roots beneath my healing.

Your presence grounded me when I faltered and helped me find my way back to hope. Because of you, I remembered my strength and learned that even in the darkest moments, love and support can light the path forward.

To the teachers who truly saw me, who recognised my potential and offered words of encouragement when hope felt distant, your belief in me kindled a spark that helped carry me forward. Your kindness and support gave me hope and reminded me of my own worth, even during the darkest moments.

A Shared Story of Love and Transformation

This story belongs to all of us. The love we share is genuine, and together we have reclaimed a life once marked by sorrow and transformed it into something beautiful and enduring.